SAFETY
PLANNING
WITH
BATTERED
WOMEN

Sage Series on Violence Against Women

Series Editors

Claire M. Renzetti
St. Joseph's University

Jeffrey L. Edleson
University of Minnesota

SAFETY PLANNING WITH BATTERED WOMEN

Complex Lives/Difficult Choices

Jill Davies
Greater Hartford Legal Assistance, Inc.

Eleanor Lyon
Diane Monti-Catania

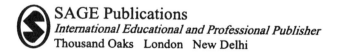

Sage Series on Violence Against Women

SAGE Publications
International Educational and Professional Publisher
Thousand Oaks   London   New Delhi

For information:

 SAGE Publications, Inc.
2455 Teller Road
Thousand Oaks, California 91320
E-mail: order@sagepub.com

SAGE Publications Ltd.
6 Bonhill Street
London EC2A
4PU United Kingdom

SAGE Publications India Pvt. Ltd.
M-32 Market
Greater Kailash I
New Delhi 110 048 India

Printed in the United States of America

Library of Congress Cataloging-in-Publication Data

Davies, Jill M.
　　Safety planning with battered women: Complex lives/difficult
choices / by Jill M. Davies, Eleanor Lyon, and Diane Monti-Catania
　　　　p.　cm. — (Sage series on violence against women; v. 7)
　　Includes bibliographical references and index.
　　0-7619-1224-X (cloth: acid-free paper) —
　　0-7619-1225-8 (pbk.: acid-free paper).
　　1. Abused women—Counseling of.　2. Social work with women.
　　3. Wife abuse—Prevention—Decision making.　4. Risk management.
　　5. Social advocacy.　I. Lyon, Eleanor.　II. Monti-Catania, Diane.
　　III. Title.　IV. Series.
　　HV1444.D38　1998
　　362.82′927—dc21　　　　　　　　　　　　　　　　　97-45282

This book is printed on acid-free paper.

03　10　9　8　7　6

Acquiring Editor:	C. Terry Hendrix
Editorial Assistant:	Dale Mary Grenfell
Production Editor:	Sherrise M. Purdum
Production Assistant:	Karen Wiley
Copy Editor:	Deirdre M. Greene
Typesetter/Designer:	Janelle LeMaster
Indexer:	Juniee Oneida
Print Buyer:	Anna Chin

To Battered Women

Contents

Preface

The revelation that advocacy with battered women needed to change began in 1986, shortly after passage of mandatory arrest provisions in Connecticut, as Jill Davies trained and provided legal consultation to advocates and Eleanor Lyon studied the new role of family violence victim advocates in court. Development of the woman-defined approach to advocacy began with the support of the Connecticut Coalition Against Domestic Violence in 1988 as part of the Model Court Response Project, which provided the opportunity to study and consider the court's response to family violence cases. Three key lessons we learned from battered women during this project were: 1) not all women involved in the legal system wanted to be; 2) some women were going to stay in their relationships; and 3) not all women could benefit from their partner's arrest, protective orders, and other court responses. These realizations led to an extensive exploration of the proper role of advocacy.

One result of this exploration was Jill Davies' development of advocacy materials and training for the family violence victim advocates who worked in court. The core concepts of woman-defined advocacy were formulated as part of this early work, known as *safety planning*. Jill was the catalyst for the development and evolution of woman-defined advocacy; through her work with battered women and advocates, her writing and analysis, she continues to lead the exploration and refinement of this approach to advocacy.

The early work on woman-defined advocacy was informed by Eleanor Lyon's research and analysis. Eleanor evaluated the first pilot testing of materials and training and provided research support to the training and evaluation of the follow-up work with advocates using the approach. Eleanor has played an ongoing significant role in woman-defined advocacy as a community researcher, offering information, analysis, and support as the training and development of woman-defined advocacy has proceeded. Some of the most meaningful information in this book came from Eleanor's interviews with battered women done as part of formal court-related research projects. Eleanor also placed the woman-defined advocacy model into the context of the current literature and thinking about family violence, battered women, and advocates.

Diane Monti-Catania joined the work on woman-defined advocacy in 1993 as a cotrainer in a statewide initiative sponsored by the Connecticut Coalition Against Domestic Violence to bring the safety planning model to all advocates working in Connecticut's domestic violence projects. Diane continued to work with advocates on the implementation of this approach. She has brought these concepts to other arenas, including the HIV/AIDS community, law enforcement, and health professionals. It was Diane's belief that the ideas contained in woman-defined advocacy be put forth in a book. Diane worked hard on early drafts of this manuscript, and actively participated in many of the conversations that led to elaboration of the model presented here.

We are grateful to the many people who helped us:

- Battered women, who courageously plan for their safety as advocates continue to try to find the answers; the lessons we learned from battered women are the basis of our approach and inform this book.
- Advocates, for trusting us to try the approach, working with us to enhance it, and the incredible, meaningful work they do with battered women.
- Anne Menard, for her vision and support of the work from its inception. Anne's unique skills and commitment provided a forum in which the approach evolved. She offered ongoing critical feedback that raised crucial questions about the broader implications of the approach. She also provided significant comments regarding the final version of the book.
- Sue Osthoff, for reading and for her thoughtful analysis and tireless support.

- Susan Schechter, for her important suggestions on the final manuscript and her contribution to the development of the list of factors and circumstances regarding the risk of life-threatening violence.
- Martie Boyer, for her analysis and support.
- Clint Sanders, for his understanding and encouragement.
- Joe, Joey, and Andrew Catania, for their unwavering support.
- Connecticut Coalition Against Domestic Violence, for its ongoing commitment to the implementation of woman-defined advocacy.
- Greater Hartford Legal Assistance (GHLA), for providing Jill the opportunity to do this work and write this book.
- Stephen Frazzini, Executive Director of GHLA, for his vision and his understanding that the pursuit of justice requires a broad view of lawyering.
- The Village for Families and Children, for its support of research and its work to end violence against women and children.
- Claire Renzetti and Jeff Edelson, for their thoughtful guidance and encouragement throughout this process.
- Nora Lester, Steve Eppler-Epstein, and Sheridan Haines, for reading and commenting on various drafts.
- Greater Hartford Legal Assistance, Inc. thanks Eleanor who will generously donate her share of the authors' proceeds to GHLA. These funds will be combined with Jill's proceeds from the book to further GHLA's mission to achieve equal justice for poor people, to work with clients to promote social justice, and to address the symptoms and root causes of poverty. We also thank the law firm of Shipman & Goodwin for its representation of GHLA, particularly attorneys Christine S. Horrigan and Theodore M. Space.
- Our partners, family, and friends. We couldn't have done it without you.

1

Introduction

Overview of Woman-Defined Advocacy

Changes in the response to family violence have been dramatic and far-reaching. A once private, almost invisible reality is now a public concern exhibited by legal, medical, and community initiatives. Training workshops and conferences about family violence are numerous. Family violence task forces and coordinating councils are forming in many communities. The connections among family violence issues and other social issues, such as youth violence, poverty, unemployment, and child abuse, are being explored. Funding has increased and a greater variety of programs is providing more services. Domestic violence is now seen as a serious problem that many people are trying to solve. The new programs and initiatives seek to identify domestic violence routinely and to respond effectively to enhance victim safety.

Yet, in spite of the goodwill and efforts, there is still no proven approach to end domestic violence for all battered women. Truly comprehensive responses are still in the planning stages. Evaluations of batterer treatment programs show mixed results. The consequences of mandatory arrest and prosecution are still being explored. Recent discussion about the effects of battering indicate complex variables and consequences for each battered woman. The negative effects of domestic violence on children are now accepted as part of the problem to be solved. Yet, current child protection strategies do not provide

1

the solution. A great deal has been accomplished in a relatively short time, but there is still a long way to go.

As the search for solutions to end domestic violence continues, battered women must cope with each experiment. Each change can bring new options and new challenges. For individual battered women, each option presented and each service provided has a consequence. Arrest could stop the attack, but end privacy or result in the woman's arrest as well. Custody orders may lead to some stability for the children, but could also result in visitation that places them in danger. Leaving might reduce the violence, but could lead to homelessness and loneliness. The pursuit of any option could bring on an escalation of the violence. Advocates are the key to helping women assess the consequences of available options and choose among them.

In this book, we use a broad definition of *advocate* to mean anyone who responds directly to help battered women in an organizational context. This can include staff or volunteers of a battered woman's shelter or program, or medical, legal, social service, law enforcement, or other institutional system that responds to domestic violence. Advocates for battered women can develop the skills and knowledge they need through experience, training, and ongoing efforts to improve. Formal education may be part of this training, but is no guarantee of effective advocacy. Effective advocates can come from diverse backgrounds and work in a variety of settings. Changes in recent years have increased the opportunities and challenges for advocates as well. Once found primarily in local domestic violence shelters, advocates are now involved in every aspect of the family violence response. The role of advocacy is affected, in part, by the context in which it occurs. Does the advocate work for the court or a local domestic violence shelter? Is the advocate part of the emergency room staff or the psychiatric unit? Different contexts provide diverse theoretical approaches to family violence and multiple, sometimes conflicting goals, for advocacy. For example, should the advocate assist in prosecuting a batterer, even if the prosecution jeopardizes a woman's physical safety? The services available in a particular context may also shape the advocacy, with advocates focusing on the use of those services to help a battered woman.

New settings for advocacy bring advocates into contact with a variety of battered women. The women who call a domestic violence shelter are actively seeking help from an advocate, and in some way see themselves as connected to the issue of domestic violence. An advocate in a health care or legal setting will meet some women who do not want help and do not identify in any way with domestic violence or battering. These women may see problems in their relationship, but do not see domestic violence advocacy as relevant.

As battered women analyze the risks they and their children face, some will conclude that physical violence is not their greatest risk, whereas others will conclude that leaving increases their risks. Much of the current response to domestic violence focuses almost exclusively on physical violence as the priority and leaving as the primary safety strategy. How can advocates bridge these gaps in perspective?

This book presents an approach to advocacy that builds a partnership between advocates and battered women, and ultimately has each battered woman defining the advocacy and help she needs. This approach, *woman-defined advocacy,* is offered not only as a way to help all women but as the necessary response to domestic violence itself.

The focus of this book is on advocacy for battered women. Although some men may be battered by a male or female partner, the overwhelming majority of domestic violence victims are women. Children can also be affected by domestic violence; safety and advocacy for children are also discussed, although primarily in the context of advocacy for their mothers. Because this approach to advocacy responds to the unique perspectives and resources of each victim, the principles should help advocates provide sensitive, meaningful advocacy for male victims. Work with men is an important part of domestic violence advocacy, but raises significant issues beyond the scope of this book.

Domestic violence is defined as a pattern of coercive control characterized by the use of physical, sexual, and psychologically abusive behaviors (Warshaw & Ganley, 1995). A batterer uses whatever strategies are necessary to control his partner. These might include physical violence, threats about the children, limits on his partner's independence, or devaluing his partner's thoughts, feelings, opinions, and dreams—her very being. At the core of this control is the batterer's goal to be the decision maker, the one who knows best, the one with the power. The woman is left with limited freedom to make decisions about her life.

In contrast, the response to domestic violence must be built on the premise that women will have the opportunity to make decisions about that response—to guide the direction and define the advocacy. This means advocacy that starts from the woman's perspective, integrates the advocate's knowledge and resources into the woman's framework, and ultimately values her thoughts, feelings, opinions, and dreams—

that she is the decision maker, the one who knows best, the one with the power. This is woman-defined advocacy.

Woman-defined advocacy is more than just a theoretical antidote to domestic violence. It provides a pragmatic approach to working with battered women that acknowledges and builds on women's perceptions and responses to their partners' power and control. Woman-defined advocacy does not ensure that a battered woman or her children will be safe—rather, it seeks to craft the alternatives that will enhance women's safety, given the realities facing each battered woman. It is not the goal of woman-defined advocacy that women should stay in violent relationships, but when staying provides the best possible alternative, woman-defined advocacy supports a woman's decision and works with her to keep her and her children as safe as possible. Until all systems respond sympathetically and effectively for all battered women, and until batterers stop battering, the response to battered women must acknowledge these limitations and the realities of women's lives. Woman-defined advocacy is advocacy for the real— not the ideal—world and for women with real, not stereotypic, lives. Woman-defined advocates who work with individual battered women to enhance their safety will not passively accept the real but limited choices for women. Systemic advocacy to improve local agency and policy responses to domestic violence is an integral part of woman-defined advocacy.

This book is divided into three parts, each reflecting a major element of woman-defined advocacy: 1) understanding a battered woman's perspective, including her risk analysis and safety plan; 2) building partnerships with battered women; and 3) systems advocacy.

In the first part of the book, "Understanding Battered Women's Perspectives," we discuss the uniqueness of each battered woman's experience with violence and provide a framework for advocates to understand battered women's analyses of the risks they face from the batterer and from their own life circumstances. Woman-defined advocacy is the acknowledgment that women experience battering in the context of diverse lives. There is much more to a battered woman than the battering. She may be a mother, a worker, a person with a disability, a friend, a leader, or a sister. Violence is a part of her life; for some women, it is almost their whole existence, whereas for others it may be a very small part. The label *battered woman* describes only one aspect of a woman who is battered.

Woman-defined advocacy acknowledges and builds on battered women's ongoing analyses of what we call *batterer-generated risks*. Batterer-generated risks are those dangers that result from the batterer's control of his partner. Battered women's analyses of batterer-generated risks include dangers other than physical violence, and consider the effects staying in or leaving their relationships have on those risks. Woman-defined advocacy does not stop at the question "Should I stay or should I go?" Instead, it adds the consideration of consequences women and children face when answering that simple question. A woman might ask, "Should I leave and risk losing my children in a custody fight?" This is the kind of question women ask themselves as they analyze their lives, options, and future; these are the issues that woman-defined advocacy must acknowledge. In addition, woman-defined advocacy anticipates that battered women will change their decisions; it allows for flexibility. Woman-defined advocacy acknowledges that battered women's risk analyses are ongoing, and shift when women get new information.

Woman-defined advocacy also acknowledges battered women's consideration of what we call *life-generated risks*. A battered woman's partner is not the sole source of risks. Life-generated risks and circumstances are aspects of battered women's lives over which they may have limited control, such as physical and mental health, financial limitations, or racism or other discrimination. We discuss some of the ways batterers may use these life-generated risks to further their control.

We identify the characteristics of the complex and creative safety plans battered women develop and use to reduce the risks they and their children face. *Safety planning* is a familiar term to most advocates. It commonly refers to a discussion between an advocate and a battered woman about her partner's physical violence, leading to a plan for her to separate from him immediately. However, battered women's safety planning begins before their contact with an advocate; it begins with their first response to batterer-generated and life-generated risks. Woman-defined advocacy builds on these safety plans.

For those advocates who approach their advocacy from an empowerment model, the principles of woman-defined advocacy will sound familiar. Such advocates may be quick to say, "I already do that." Yet, as advocates explore both the theory and the practice of woman-defined advocacy, they may find they need to change their approach— to make a shift—to provide advocacy defined by the woman. For example, many battered women do not see physical violence as their primary risk or leaving as their most viable option. Accepting this reality will be a shift for some advocates because much of the response to domestic violence assumes incorrectly that battered women's greatest concern is their partners' physical violence and that leaving will reduce that risk. We discuss how working with battered women who remain in their relationships challenges advocates to develop new ways of thinking about how they do the work and how they define success.

In the second part, "Building Partnerships With Battered Women," we discuss the importance of an advocate's knowledge, experience, and analysis to woman-defined advocacy. We describe how to build partnerships with battered women that provide advocates with the opportunity to integrate their knowledge, resources, and advocacy into the woman's risk analysis and plans. This integration provides both the advocate and the battered woman with the best possible information on which to base further analysis and safety planning.

Woman-defined advocacy is not the blind, passive acceptance of a battered woman's choices or analysis. We discuss how an advocate's review of a battered woman's risk analysis will further the integration of the advocate's and the woman's knowledge. A thorough risk review requires a delicate balance between adding to and enhancing the information a woman provides and completely replacing the woman's judgment. We stress the importance of including life-threatening violence and risks to children in every review and provide advocates with approaches for doing so.

Woman-defined advocacy can seem hard to do every time with each battered woman. In this book, we discuss some of the key challenges. There are batterers who do not stop, women and children who are injured, limited time and resources, racism and other discrimination, and systems that devalue the role of advocacy. As advocates grapple with these issues, they may rely on a more service-defined approach as a way to cope. When advocates focus exclusively on providing a service, whether or not it fits into a battered woman's risk analysis or safety plans, they are providing what we call *service-defined advocacy*. Although providing services is an essential part of the work of all domestic violence advocates, we stress that providing services should be distinguished from advocacy defined by services. We also discuss other challenges to understanding a battered woman's perspective, such as those that result from differences in background, life experience, and language. In Chapter 7, "Safety Planning With Battered Women," we discuss how advocates can work with battered women to strengthen their safety plans.

In Part III, "Systems Advocacy," we discuss the importance of creating a supportive work environment so individual woman-defined advocacy can flourish. We also provide strategies for building such an environment.

In addition, we discuss the importance of policy advocacy. One of the premises of individual woman-defined advocacy is that advocates must work with the realities and options available to each woman. If a system does not respond or responds poorly, then battered women have fewer options for their safety and the safety of their children. Therefore, a natural part of advocacy for individual battered women is advocacy to enhance systemic responses to all battered women. The more and better options available, the more likely battered women and their children will be safe. Policy advocacy in the legal, health, government, mental health, child protection, and social service systems is an integral part of woman-defined advocacy.

About the Format of This Book

We've tried to make the book accessible to the variety of communities working on family violence issues. The format provides a theoretical discussion of woman-defined advocacy, along with practical "how-to" information. Brief summaries of relevant research on battered women, domestic violence, and advocacy are integrated throughout the book. Each chapter includes a section outlining the elements of woman-defined advocacy. Figure 1.1 summarizes all the elements. The examples used in this book, although based on knowledge from years of advocacy and research, are hypothetical.

Why We Wrote This Book

Woman-defined advocacy builds on the historic commitment of the battered women's movement to empower battered women. We believe advocacy is essential to battered women's safety and well-being. Advocates provide strength, comfort, and life-saving support to battered women and their children. In an age of protective orders, specialized units, and coordinating councils, we have sometimes forgotten the importance of simply listening to battered women. Listening alone will not end domestic violence, nor will woman-defined advocacy. There is a great deal we need to learn about battered women and the best approaches to advocacy. We hope this book will help advocates help battered women.

1. Understand a battered woman's perspective, including her risk analysis and safety plan.
   - Understand a battered woman's risk analysis.
     - Identify the range of batterer-generated risks in a woman's analysis.
     - Identify the effect of staying or leaving on those risks.
   - Understand how life-generated risks affect a battered woman's risk analysis and plans.
     - Identify how her abusive partner may manipulate such risks to further his control.
   - Understand a battered woman's past and current safety plans.
     - Identify staying, leaving, and protection strategies.
     - Identify the time frame for a woman's current plans.
2. Build a partnership with a battered woman.
   - Respectfully review a battered woman's risk analysis.
     - Review for life-threatening violence.
     - Review risks to children.
   - Work with a battered woman to strengthen her safety plan.
     - Identify available and relevant options and resources.
     - Analyze these options with the battered woman.
     - Develop and implement the refined safety plan.
     - Provide enhanced advocacy when needed, and in all cases of life-threatening violence.
3. Provide systemic woman-defined advocacy.
   - Build a woman-defined advocacy environment.
     - Choose an approach.
     - Establish the elements of a woman-defined advocacy environment.
       - Demonstrate a commitment to provide woman-defined advocacy.
       - Define the role of the advocate broadly enough, and give advocates the freedom, time, resources, and support to respond to the uniqueness and complexity of battered women.
       - Pursue strong collaborative working relationships with other agencies while maintaining battered woman's privacy.
   - Provide woman-defined policy advocacy to further individual woman-defined advocacy and enhance the safety of all battered women.
     - Gather information and determine who needs to be involved in the process.
     - Analyze and review the information gathered.
     - Develop a position based on the analysis and plan how to implement it.
     - Monitor and enhance the plan by continuing the information gathering, analysis, and strategizing.

Figure 1.1. Elements of Woman-Defined Advocacy

PART I

UNDERSTANDING BATTERED WOMEN'S PERSPECTIVES

Part I is about the image and reality of battered women's lives. The focus is on how battered women analyze the dangers they face and how they make decisions and plans for their safety. This part begins with an exploration of the public image of battered women. The following chapters explore the complexity of battered women's experiences and how advocates can discover each battered woman's unique perspective. These chapters discuss what research and advocacy experience have taught us so far, how advocates can find out about the individual woman they are working with, and how advocates can most effectively use that information to advance women's own plans and priorities.

2

Creating the Image
of Battered Women

Great strides have been made in organized efforts to combat
relationship violence against women in the past 20 years. Concerned
advocates have increased public awareness and understanding, obtained ongoing funding for temporary shelters in most states, changed
laws and policies to enhance the responsiveness of major social
institutions, and provided specialized training for those who work
with battered women and their abusers. These accomplishments have
encouraged women who have experienced violence in their relationships to come forward and seek help and support in growing numbers
every year.

At the same time, knowledge about the dynamics of family violence against women has accumulated rapidly, as practitioners have
gained experience and researchers have completed increasingly so-
phisticated studies. These successes have been accompanied by sky-
rocketing demands on the legal, advocacy, medical, and therapeutic
systems, however. These institutions, in turn, have often responded to
escalating demand in bureaucratic ways, partly because of the formal
limitations in the services they offer, and partly because they do not
have sufficient resources to meet everyone's needs.

The tensions between the volume and complexity of battered
women's needs and available institutional responses have also high-
lighted debates and conflicts among advocates and other practitioners
that have existed since the beginning of the battered women's move-

ment. The debates focus on the most appropriate ways to interpret battered women's behavior and corresponding strategies for working with battered women to promote their safety most effectively. The language used, the intensity of discussion, and the implications for work with women and resources have varied over the past 20 years, but the debates have remained.

As national models and federal policies are developed in the late 1990s, it is important to reassess approaches to intervention with battered women. In the chapters that follow, we outline a strategy that reflects accumulated knowledge and concerns raised by advocates and others since the 1970s. Each part of the overall strategy has a history and context in what is known about battered women and the best ways to work with them. This history covers, first, the early years of public awareness and the understandings of intimate violence against women that contributed to establishing shelters and other services. Additional aspects of the historical and practice context are provided in later chapters.

The Early Years

Violence against women has always existed in the United States. In the mid-20th century, changing cultural norms, prompted in part by women's increasing involvement in the paid labor force and the civil rights and women's movements, made behavior that was previously personal a matter of public concern. First child abuse, and then woman abuse, became redefined as social problems (Tierney, 1982). The first shelter for battered women and their children was established in California in 1964 through the efforts of local members of Al-Anon (Barnett & LaViolette, 1993). Subsequently, the women's movement mobilized a battered women's movement in the early 1970s, which began to create crisis hotlines, shelters, and other specialized services. By the mid-1970s, a wide range of feminist organizations was promoting public awareness and services for battered women, with substantial success.

From the start, differences in approach were apparent. These differences reflected the contrasting strategies shown by grassroots and professional activists in many arenas (Freeman, 1975; Tierney, 1982). Although there was overlap, these two groups of activists tended to differ in the extent of their formal training and credentials, the relative emphasis in their self-conception as "professionals" or "activists," and the organizational context of their work (in a shelter

or in an agency or private practice). The grassroots approach emphasized supportive, "empowering" responses offered by counselors or
advocates who saw themselves as the battered woman's peers. The
professional approach was closer to a familiar, office-based, individual
counseling or therapy model; it was often seen by advocates as more
judgmental and less egalitarian than the grassroots approach. Jennifer
Fleming (1979), who wrote one of the early works on the battered
women's movement, quotes shelter worker and movement analyst
Lisa Leghorn as saying,

> Peer counseling, whereby the "helper" identifies with the "victim,"
> constitutes a fundamental transformation in the way services are
> perceived and offered. No longer is a supposedly helpless, dependent,
> ignorant and masochistic client coming to seek salvation from a
> supposedly mature, wise and all-knowing counselor. (p. 360)

Susan Schechter (1982), in a highly influential account of the movement, also quotes Leghorn to describe the grassroots approach:

> We were not providing social services. As staffers, we were not
> different from the women except that they were in crisis. We only
> gave people safety and information. We emphasized women have to
> make their own decisions. . . . If you caretake, you don't give a
> woman what she needs. (p. 67)

Schechter later describes the grassroots self-help oriented model:

> Self-help, closely related to definitions of "empowerment," is de-
> scribed as a process through which women, experts about their own
> lives, learn to know their strength. "Empowerment" combines ideas
> about internalizing personal and collective power and validating
> women's personal experiences as politically oppressive rather than
> self-caused or "crazy." (p. 109)

Both Fleming (1979) and Schechter (1982) explicitly describe
differences in approach held by professionals and grassroots activists
from the beginning. Fleming describes the differences in the two
approaches in conflictual language when she notes that activists Del
Martin and Sharon Rice Vaughn felt "that the professional 'treatment'
model automatically serves to create a barrier that further dehuman-
izes and isolates the woman who has already been victimized not only
by her violent husband or lover but by society itself " (p. 358).

Underlying the differences in approach were divergent assumptions about battered women's cognitive and coping abilities when they

reached the point of seeking help. In particular, the two approaches differed in their interpretations of battered women's decisions regarding their own safety and the future of their relationship with their partner. For example, Fleming (1979) quotes therapists Ball and Wyman:

> One of the major goals should be to increase the woman's feeling of being in control of her life. The counselor or therapist must realize that a battered woman will initially demonstrate a lack of motivation and show poor cognitive problem-solving skills. The therapy process must begin with a very directive approach. . . . Despite assertiveness training, individual and group therapy, some battered women will choose to stay in the battering relationship. The counselors should help the client explore the rationale for this decision to determine if the reasons are realistic or mythical. (p. 100)

As this excerpt illustrates, a woman's decision to remain in the relationship with her abuser was often regarded, particularly by professionals, as an indication that she was unable to make decisions in her own interest. Schechter (1982) summarizes and highlights these aspects of the difference in approach:

> Professionals and self-help advocates disagree on how skills should be acquired, who is the expert, and what kind of experience heals. Self-help advocates stress that battered women, those who know what it is like to be beaten, are the experts who can best help one another. While some professionals agree, many claim that specialized knowledge and status gives them authority over their clients and means that they know best. (pp. 109-110)
>
> Battered women are not passive; rather, they engage in step-like, logical behavior as they attempt to stop the violence or leave. Not all of them are successful because the major variable, the violent man, is outside their realm of control. Staying, especially given the lack of resources and social supports for leaving, should never be read as accepting violence. (p. 233)

Shelter programs relied on dedicated volunteers and staff who did not demand large salaries for their work. Most operated from self-help, peer support models of intervention. From the beginning of the work with battered women, however, approaches espoused by more therapeutically oriented professionals were also advocated. As time went on, these clinical understandings of battered women's behavior and decision making gained popularity both within and outside the movement.

By the early 1980s, several analysts had noted this trend with some alarm (e.g., Johnson, 1981; Tierney, 1982). Schechter (1982) is not alone in ascribing much of this change to the influence of needed funders:

> In approaching funders and community groups, activists encountered charitable and professional values that emphasized helping the "needy" and often unwittingly assigned to women the permanent status of helpless "victim." The pervasive influence of psychological explanations for social problems was seen as funding agency after funding agency defined battered women as a mental health issue. (p. 95)

Similarly, Liane Davis (1987) expresses concern that social workers could be moving toward an "unrealistic perspective by focusing attention on treatment for the individual and the couple and minimizing the importance of the sociopolitical context within which the problem exists" (p. 311).

The Public Construction of "The Battered Woman"

During the early years of the battered women's movement, advocates needed to focus some of their energies on convincing the public and policymakers that battering was a serious problem that affected many women from all walks of life. Supportive resources were limited; policies did not recognize that battering was a social, not individual "family" problem; and popular understandings often cast battered women as masochists who "asked" for the violence they experienced. Advocates needed to construct a public image of "the battered woman" who was more sympathetic.

As part of their effort to generate broad-based support, advocates publicly emphasized a model of battered women as "pure victims."[1] The model has several components. First, abused women are not themselves violent, unless driven to violence in self-defense. Second, battered women are characterized as having experienced extreme physical violence separated by periods of emotional abuse. Third, the abuse is presented as a pattern of events that necessarily increase in severity and frequency, and that will only get worse unless someone intervenes. Finally, battered women are described as terrified by this experience.

This image accurately describes many, but not all of the battered women who sought shelter and other help during the 1970s and early

1980s. During the 1980s, however, substantial institutional changes were adopted across the country, particularly in the law enforcement and court systems. These changes were a result of several sources of effort. First, people involved in the battered women's movement lobbied vigorously for stable funding and laws that would increase police responsiveness to calls for help. Shelter staff across the country had encountered legions of women who had found the police response to be slow, inconsistent, and unlikely to result in formal action except in cases of the most severe and visible injury.

Second, researchers and advocates combined to urge reform of police practice (e.g., Horton, Simonidis, & Simonidis, 1987; Lerman, 1986). Their efforts received support from the widely publicized results of the Minneapolis Police Experiment (Sherman & Berk, 1984), which indicated that arrest was the police response most associated with lower rates of subsequent reports of violence (compared with mediation or temporary separation to cool off).

Third, national media attention and public outcry followed several cases in which the police failed to provide an adequate response, and the battered woman involved was killed or seriously injured (see Jones, 1994, for several prominent cases). One of the most influential of these cases led to a successful lawsuit against the local police department. Within a year after Tracey Thurman was awarded nearly $2 million in damages, the Connecticut legislature passed one of the most comprehensive mandatory arrest laws in the nation. By the end of the decade, several other states had passed laws requiring or encouraging arrest in family violence incidents when there was probable cause.

Passage of these laws contributed to an environment of escalating change in policy and procedures for responding to battered women. The publicity surrounding the legal advocacy efforts, announcements of research results, and the Thurman case enhanced visibility and spread information about battering, particularly in its most extreme forms. These efforts also provided essential information to women about options available in their communities. Coupled with invigorated arrest policies, public education campaigns contributed to more women seeking help, support, or redress from the courts, shelter programs, or other social service agencies.

The public image of battering remained much as it had been in the late 1970s and early 1980s, and this image provided the foundation for the specific services, policies, remedies, and protocols that were developed. The policy and practice changes meant, however, that the women who came to the attention of advocates and service providers were more diverse than before and their experiences varied from the profile of abused women that had developed. Because of mandatory arrest, for example, women who did not initiate help seeking found themselves talking with victim advocates or other court personnel. In addition, women who had less experience with battering or less physical injury began coming to court; women also appeared who had multiple problems in addition to the physical violence in their lives, such as drug and alcohol involvement or their own criminal activity. In short, the "real" battered women who came to public attention were more complicated and increasingly diverged from the image that had fueled public support. They were not necessarily "pure victims," nor had all of them experienced extreme physical violence or psychological abuse. They were not necessarily terrified of their abuser. Instead, they had more varied sets of experience and needs for assistance, protection, and support, which they understood in complex ways. This growing complexity has required that advocates think about their work with battered women in more flexible ways than before, particularly in the context of the growing use of service-defined advocacy.

The History of Service-Defined Advocacy

Service-defined advocacy, in which advocates fit women into the services available without understanding their plans, has become widespread over time, almost without anyone realizing it. It has emerged partly as a result of three related developments over the past 15 years. First, grassroots advocates and others have had "success" in changing a variety of public policies; some of these, such as policies that encourage or require arrest in battering incidents, have dramatically increased the numbers of women seeking help or support. Second, service-defined advocacy has become more widespread, ironically, because of public education and the campaigns to accomplish these policy changes, and the construction of the image of "the battered woman." These efforts, too, have contributed to increased numbers of women coming forward. Third, the climate of policy change has made research easier to conduct: More funding became available, research populations became more accessible, and more precise questions emerged as diverse service providers sought ways to intervene with battered women and their abusers most effectively, and researchers evaluated their efforts. These three developments led ultimately to widespread overgeneralizations about battered women and related policy and advocacy problems for several reasons.

First, the numbers of women coming forward, especially to courts and shelters, were sometimes overwhelming to already crowded systems. These expanding numbers, and the growing diversity of issues and needs presented by the women, often added to the frustration experienced by the advocates and other service providers who worked with battered women. Many women did not comply with institutional protocols, were not grateful for the "help" they were offered, generally did not conform to agency images of "good clients" because they were trying to deal with multiple issues (which did not match the constructed image), and often returned to their abusing partners despite program efforts. Due to insufficient resources, courts and shelter staff were faced with the necessity of choosing the women who would receive the most time and attention; the women who looked most like the constructed image of battered women were most likely to be chosen.

Loseke (1992) summarizes the outcome of this selection process in the shelter she studied:

> The world thus was practically and rhetorically divided into two types of people. Women were "battered" or "non-battered"; all heterogeneity disappeared. So, regardless of how these petitioners [for shelter services] differed among themselves, on-the-record all new clients were instances of the same type of person: the "battered woman." (p. 94)

When women were seen through this kind of single lens, they were also seen as needing the same types of services. Similar ways of categorizing women and their needs have been found in other shelters as well (e.g., McKeel & Sporakowski, 1993).

Service providers in other settings—such as the courts (Emerson, 1994; Lyon & Mace, 1991) and public health (e.g., Campbell, 1991)—have been found to focus on trying to fit battered women into the services available in similar ways. Warshaw (1993; see also Kurz, 1987; Stark, Flitcraft, & Frazier, 1979) is particularly clear about how the medical model's categories contributed to a service-defined approach, and its effect on battered women in a large urban hospital emergency room:

> The dynamics of an abusive relationship are recreated in an encounter in which the subjectivity and needs of the woman are reduced to [service] categories that meet the needs of another, not her own, a relationship in which she as a person is neither seen nor heard. . . . In this setting, where large numbers of patients must be seen expedi-

tiously, it is the medical model that predominates. . . . The medical model, in fact, can only "medicalize," reduce things to categories it can handle and control. (pp. 142-143)

Eisikovits and Buchbinder (1996) describe a similar process operating in battered women's encounters with their social workers. In this case, however, the social workers' approach led the women to try to fit themselves to the services:

> [The battered women] were forced to think simultaneously of what they wanted to report and how it would be heard by the social worker—their audience. In such cases, the women felt they were not true to themselves. They were what they were expected to be. They learned to tell an unassailable story. (Eisikovits & Buchbinder, 1996, p. 433)

Second, overgeneralizations about the battered woman were spurred on by the types of research projects undertaken. The initial emphasis on reform of the legal system contributed to research not only on the characteristics of people who came to court because of abuse and the usefulness of alternative responses (e.g., Buzawa & Buzawa, 1990, 1993; Dutton, 1988; Hilton, 1993), but also on the effectiveness of treatment programs. Efforts to identify factors that could predict successful legal or clinical interventions for both battered women and their abusive partners encouraged research that focused on individual (especially pathological) characteristics to explain behavior and outcomes.

At the same time, attempts to use the *battered woman syndrome* as support for a defense for abused women who assault or kill their batterers contributed to more widespread adoption of the syndrome and the often-related concepts of learned helplessness, posttraumatic stress disorder (PTSD), and the cycle of violence as primary ways to understand battered women and explain their behavior. This development spawned further research on the syndrome, such that it became one of the primary models, part of "what we all know" about battered women (e.g., Dutton & Painter, 1993; Koss, Goodman, Browne, Fitzgerald, Keita, & Russo, 1994; Walker, 1991; Whalen, 1996), although its overuse and accuracy have been challenged recently (Dutton, 1996a, b). Finally, overacceptance of the syndrome model suggested that women themselves may not be the best judges of their situation, and that the "experts" in shelters, the courts, and psychological treatment settings need to help them interpret their experience and construct the best plans (Cahn & Meier, 1995).

The combination of large numbers of women seeking help and research that focused on individual syndrome-related explanations of women's behavior helped to make a service-defined approach seem appropriate. The resulting image of the battered woman was often overgeneralized to most women who sought help—especially by staff in organizations that did not have the time or energy for complex individual assessments. Loseke (1992) describes the effect of such images on shelter workers' perceptions of battered women: "The battered woman is constructed as a type of woman who is emotionally confused and therefore unable to define leaving as her most reasonable course of action" (p. 27). She continues much later,

> If clients offered alternative definitions of themselves perhaps it was only because these women had been "brainwashed.". . . Workers believed [battered women] were prone to "denial" or "ambivalence," and that such emotions should be transformed to those properly expected of a woman who had been repeatedly and viciously assaulted: anger and sadness. (p. 102)

Similarly, O'Brien and Murdock (1993), in a study of shelter workers, found that workers viewed battered women who thought the abuse might stop much less positively than those who thought it would continue. The women who did not think the abuse might stop were considered most likely to leave their partner, and therefore most responsive to the help the workers could provide. Such battered women fit the model of the woman who would take advantage of the services available, were more well liked by the workers, and were therefore more likely to get the most help.

Ironically, then, widespread institutional changes have had several results. Vital new supports and expanded options were developed for battered women. At the same time, psychological models for understanding their behavior gained sufficient prominence that the women who did not make the decisions and changes intended by the policies were sometimes seen as damaged and lacking credibility. This, coupled with the limited resources available and limited coordination among the various organizations battered women turned to, contributed to the expansion of service-defined advocacy.

Note

1. See Loseke (1992, pp. 14-20) for an extended analysis of the image of the battered woman most commonly used as part of advocacy for increased programs and services and policy change.

3

Batterer-Generated Risks

Batterers use physical violence and a variety of tactics to control their partners. As battered women experience these tactics, they analyze them and identify which pose particular risks for them. The risks women face go beyond the possibility of injury from physical violence. When battered women analyze their risks, they consider a broad range of abusive behaviors, both physical and nonphysical. Battered women also think about their children: "Do they hear the fights?" "How will this affect their futures?" Battered women are concerned about whether or not they will be able keep their jobs, how the bills will get paid, and what people will think of them if they find out they are battered. As battered women consider the range of risks, they might ask themselves the same question that is so often asked of them: "Why do I stay?"

When battered women ask themselves about staying, however, the questions are more complete and cover the range of possible implications for their lives. They think about what they have to gain or lose by staying in or leaving the relationship and weigh the risks or consequences they may face if they do try to leave. The questions battered women ask themselves will sound more like the following: "Should I leave and risk losing my children in a custody fight?" "If I stay, will he start to hit the children?" "If I try to get out, will he find me and fulfill his threat to kill me?" "Should I leave and risk living with my children in poverty?"

This chapter explores the first of three aspects of battered women's perspectives: the analysis of *batterer-generated* risks. Batterer-generated risks are those dangers that result from the batterer's control of his partner. Battered women's analyses of batterer-generated risks include identifying the range of risks they and their children face and a consideration of how staying in or leaving their relationships might affect those risks. The other two aspects of battered women's perspectives discussed in this book are life-generated risks and battered women's decision making about safety planning. These topics are discussed in Chapter 4, "Life-Generated Risks," and Chapter 5, "Battered Women's Decision Making and Safety Plans."

The majority of batterer-generated risks that battered women identify as part of their risk analysis can be broken down into seven broad categories: 1) physical injury, 2) psychological harm, 3) risks to and involving the children, 4) financial risks, 5) risk to or about family and friends, 6) loss of relationship, and 7) risks involving arrest or legal status. This chapter explores each of these categories by discussing what research can tell us, describing some of the types of risks battered women might identify in each category, and how battered women might consider the effects of staying or leaving on those risks. The last section of this chapter describes advocacy strategies for understanding battered women's perspectives on batterer-generated risks. Additional information regarding risks and advocacy, with a particular focus on lethality and risks to children, is included in Chapter 6, "Risk Analysis," and Chapter 7, "Safety Planning With Battered Women."

Risk of Physical Injury

Physical injuries—black eyes, bruised faces and bodies, broken bones, stitches, and wounds—are the most visible and clearly identified risks to a battered woman. A batterer uses a wide range of physical attacks to control his partner. This might include shoving her, shaking her, slapping her, kicking her, punching her, pulling her by her hair, burning her, using items around the house to hit her, using weapons such as guns and knives to threaten or hurt her, and trying to kill her. Physical attacks can include sexual violence, including forced sexual intercourse or other sexual activities, which may also include the risk of HIV or other sexually transmitted diseases. In addition to the injuries inflicted directly by the batterer, a woman may face a range of secondary physical problems related to the assault, such as headaches, dizziness, or sleeplessness.

As battered women incorporate the consideration of staying in or leaving their relationship, they may consider whether leaving will increase or decrease the physical and sexual violence. Some batterers have made it clear to their partners that if they leave, they will find them and really hurt them or even try to kill them. For some women, this is a threat they may or may not have tested. Other battered women may have tried to leave before and they will factor into their analysis how their abusive partners acted last time.

Of all the risks to battered women that stem directly from their partners' efforts to control them, physical violence has received the most research, policy, and media attention (Crowell & Burgess, 1996). Information has been collected from women who go to shelters, women who seek help from mental health clinics or hospitals, and community and national surveys, among other sources.

The accumulated evidence shows that physical violence is widespread, varies in severity, and is often repeated. The most widely cited national surveys (Straus & Gelles, 1986) have found, for example, that more than 11% of women experienced some form of violence at the hands of their male partners during the 12 months prior to the interview; 3% of women experienced what the researchers called *severe violence* (kicked, hit with a fist, beaten up, threatened, or hurt with a weapon) during that same period. The surveys also found that the physical violence was often repeated: of those who reported any violence, 19% said there had been two incidents, 16% stated there had been three or four incidents, and 32% revealed five or more violent episodes. In addition, the surveys found that such experiences were shared by large numbers of women: More than a quarter of the people who took part had experienced violence at some time during their current relationship.

The national random surveys have found that African Americans are more likely than Anglo Americans to say that woman abuse has occurred in an intimate relationship (Cazenave & Straus, 1990; Hampton & Gelles, 1994). Studies of the incidence of wife abuse among Hispanics and Asian Americans have varied considerably (Huisman, 1996; Perilla, Bakeman, & Norris, 1994; Sorenson, Upchurch, & Shen, 1996). Huisman (1996) reports that Asian women who are battered are more likely than other women to wait until the abuse has become a crisis before they report it. In general, however, these studies do not indicate how much of the difference could be explained by socioeconomic factors and how much could be attributed to cultural or other factors.

Some researchers have investigated the extent to which women are battered during pregnancy. One of the major national surveys (Gelles, 1988) found that 15% of the women who had been pregnant were assaulted by their partners at least once during the first half of pregnancy, and 17% were assaulted during the second half of pregnancy. A study of 691 women at prenatal clinics found that 17% experienced physical or sexual abuse during their pregnancy (McFarlane, Parker, Soeken, & Bullock, 1992). Some medical observers have estimated that as many as 37% of obstetric patients are physically attacked by a male partner sometime during the pregnancy (Helton, McFarlane, & Anderson, 1987). Researchers have also found that violence against women by intimate partners is not confined to the people with whom they live. A study of 2,602 women from 32 colleges and universities, for example, found that 32% reported aggression at the hands of a date or other intimate (White & Koss, 1991).

The primary national surveys of adult couples did not ask questions about sexually abusive acts, but other research has explored this issue. Although some research has found rates of sexual assault as "low" as 20%, partly due to who was asked and how the questions were phrased, the studies that have approached these questions with the greatest sensitivity have found that between 34% and 59% of the women who were physically assaulted by their partners also reported being assaulted sexually. In addition, studies have found that battered women who are sexually assaulted by their partners are more likely than other abused women to experience more severe or injurious nonsexual attacks (see Koss et al., 1994, for a summary of this research).

Physical and sexual abuse by partners may increase women's risks for illnesses or aggravated medical conditions, both directly and indirectly. Studies of the medical effect of woman abuse have used different kinds of measures, none of them ideal. They do show, however, that the effect can vary from general time in bed recuperating to greater risk of life-threatening illness. A national random sample survey found, for example, that women who had experienced "severe" violence in the past year averaged twice as many days in bed "due to illness" in the previous month as those who had experienced minor violence or none at all (Gelles & Straus, 1988). A pilot study in one clinic found that between 67% and 83% of the HIV-positive women either were currently or had been in abusive relationships with men who also refused to wear condoms or provide other protection. In another random study, 45% of the women who had sexual problems and 47% of those who had other gynecological difficulties were battered women. (Both studies are cited in Warshaw & Ganley, 1995.)

Although most domestic violence against women is not "severe" and does not lead eventually to their deaths, it is still significant. In 1994, 28% of female homicide victims were killed by husbands, ex-husbands, or boyfriends. Furthermore, analysis of data over the past 20 years shows that the rate of female homicide by partners has remained stable (Bureau of Justice Statistics, 1994; Federal Bureau of Investigation, 1995). Women are much more likely than men to be killed by a current or former intimate partner. Just 3% of male homicide victims are killed by wives or girlfriends. None of these statistics from law enforcement agencies includes information about the motivations or context for these homicides.

Despite the relatively low risk of lethality, women who experience physical attacks consider the threat of life-threatening violence. Some women believe their partners will kill them. When women think they may be killed, they pay extremely careful attention to their partners' behavior and may be in the best position to determine their risk for being killed or seriously injured.

The primary patterns found in the research on the extent and severity of violence, then, show that physical violence is widespread and the majority of it does not involve "serious" physical injury, although the rates of homicide suggest that severe abuse or death can be a reasonable fear. Although many women face ongoing devastating risks, the experience of many other battered women who come to the attention of advocates and service providers does not match the popular image of a person who is subject to ever-escalating and increasing physical violence.

The popular image also neglects the substantial physical risks experienced by many women after they leave the relationship, what Mahoney (1991) calls "separation assault." Taking the steps that will end the relationship does not mean that the violence will stop. The 1993 Canadian Violence Against Women Survey, for example, found that 19% of separated wives were physically abused by their (ex-) husbands during the separation period; 35% of them maintained that their husbands had increased their violence after the separation. Ellis and Stuckless's (1992) study of couples who sought mediation for divorce-related issues reports that more than 25% of the women said their partners had abused or threatened them after they separated. Giles-Sims (1983) studied women who had left a shelter and did not return to their abusive partner and found that 44% of them had experienced violence at least once more. Arendell's (1995) study of divorced men found that 40% admitted they had threatened or become violent toward their former wives after the marriage ended. Clearly, "leaving" the relationship does not necessarily end the violence, as the following example illustrates.

Linda

Linda has been married to Frank for 4 years. Frank works as a supervisor at a local factory. He doesn't let her work or go out with her friends. He comes home from work angry and often sits in front of the TV for hours without talking. If he feels that Linda is not paying attention to him, or has fallen short on some household demand, he beats her up, punching her in the face and chest. He says he's trying to teach her a lesson about being a "good wife." After these incidents, Frank apologizes to Linda for hurting her and then insists they have sex. Linda recently told Frank that she was thinking of leaving if things didn't get better between them. Frank mocked her, saying she'd never make it on her own and that she'd be back in a day. Linda left anyway and went to a friend's house. Frank followed her and stood on the front lawn screaming that he was going to kill himself if she didn't come out to talk with him. Linda went out to calm him down. He screamed at her, "Come back with me now—if I can't have you no one will."

Linda's Risk Analysis. Linda analyzes the batterer-generated risks she faces (Figure 3.1, at the end of this chapter, provides an outline of batterer-generated risks). Her analysis includes a consideration of the effects of staying with or leaving Frank. Linda wants to leave Frank for good. But her analysis of Frank's recent behavior makes her think that leaving may increase her risks of harm. Linda's immediate concern is that she'll lose the option of staying with her friend and future support if she doesn't leave with Frank right now so he'll stop screaming in the yard. Linda has never seen Frank like this before. She doesn't know what he'll do. Linda is worried that if she tries to leave Frank for good, he might kill himself and her. On the other hand, Linda knows if she goes back to Frank and stays with him, things will be the same. She's convinced he won't change; he'll continue to be distant, control what she does, hit her, and demand sex.

Risk of Psychological Harm

Batterers also use a range of psychological tactics to undermine their partner's self-confidence and autonomy. These tactics may involve a constant barrage of insults, threats, and attacks: "putting their partners down," blaming them for anything that goes wrong, severely criticizing their parenting, calling them degrading names, and questioning their intelligence, abilities, thoughts, bodies, and sexual abilities or performance. Another tactic is to make all the decisions in the family or to prevent the woman from attending significant events. For example, a battered woman's closest relative may be the grandmother who raised her. The woman's abusive partner may keep her from visiting her grandmother in the hospital or even attending her funeral. The harm and pain of psychological attacks may be in the forefront of some battered women's risk analyses. Some batterers use their partners' mental health concerns to control them further. For example, a batterer may constantly tell his partner that she is crazy and a bad parent to devalue her thoughts and opinions and become the sole decision maker in the family. In other situations, the batterer may encourage or insist that his partner use drugs or alcohol with him and will undermine any attempt she might make to stop using.

A woman's mental health risk analysis includes the consideration of staying in or leaving the relationship. If she feels "crazy" when she is around her partner, then leaving him may lessen the feeling. If, however, she is addicted to drugs or alcohol, she will still have to face this addiction even if her partner is out of the picture, although leaving him may be a necessary step in her recovery. If a woman's mental health risk is caused by certain batterer behavior that does not cease when she leaves, then the risk may not go away. For example, a battered woman is extremely anxious and depressed because her husband has raped and beaten her many times. She has left the relationship, but he knows where she works. He stalks her and tells her that "you still belong to me and I can have you whenever I want." Leaving did not remove her anxiety or her depression.

A battered woman's ability to analyze her mental health risks may be extremely accurate or may be impaired by the risk itself. Advocacy with women facing mental health risks is discussed in more detail in Chapter 6.

Large amounts of information have begun to accumulate about the psychological risks posed to women when they have a partner who is physically abusive. Some of those risks are described as a direct result of the physical violence or coercive control itself. These may include fear, a sense of lack of control over events, depression, an inability to predict the partner's behavior, stress, hopelessness, anxiety, shame, lowered self-esteem, and alcohol and drug abuse. Other psychological risks are considered a direct result of the abusive partner's psychological abuse. Most battered women describe examples of frequent psychological abuse that occurs between physically violent episodes. Much of the research that has investigated the psychological effect of battering has not attempted to distinguish between the effects of the two types of abuse.

One important effort to investigate psychological impacts and separate the effects of different forms of abuse involved interviews about emotional abuse with 234 women who said they had been physically abused (Follingstad, Rutledge, Berg, Hause, & Polek, 1990). This study found that emotional abuse was prominent for nearly all women who were physically abused, and was often regarded by the women as more troubling. Only three of these women reported that they had never experienced emotional abuse. Seventy-two percent of the women indicated they had experienced at least four of the six types of emotional abuse studied (threats of abuse, ridicule, jealousy, threats to change the marriage, restriction, and damage to property). Nearly half of the women rated ridicule as the worst type of emotional abuse, and only restriction and jealousy occurred more often. Eighty-six percent of the women said that ridicule had a negative impact on them. Furthermore, 72% of the women in this study reported that the emotional abuse had a more severe effect on them than the physical abuse. These women were also most likely to report that the emotional abuse was increasing over time and the negative effects stemmed from the emotional abuse alone, not from its connection to any threat of physical harm.

Although they have not distinguished between the effects of physical and emotional abuse, most studies have found a relationship between the frequency and severity of abuse and psychological distress. Using one of the largest samples (3,002), Gelles and Harrop (1989) report that women who had experienced violence and abuse reported higher levels of distress than those who had not.

The national survey conducted by Gelles and Straus (1988) compared the frequency of an array of symptoms among women who had experienced "severe " violence, "minor" violence, or no violence in the previous year. The list of symptoms included headaches, cold sweats, stress or nervousness, sadness or depression, feeling too many difficulties to overcome, feeling bad or worthless, feeling unable to cope, wondering if anything was worthwhile, feeling totally hopeless, having suicidal thoughts, and attempted suicide. The women who had experienced violence in the past year were substantially more likely to have felt every one of these signs of distress "fairly often" or "very often," and those who had experienced severe violence were much more symptomatic than those who had experienced minor violence.

Clearly, research shows that most women who experience physical or psychological abuse by their partners are emotionally affected by it to some degree. The more severe the violence, the more frequently it occurs, and the longer it lasts, the greater the emotional effect is likely to be. The research indicates diverse reactions, however: The effect of abuse is not universally devastating or debilitating by any means, as the popular socially constructed image would suggest. Many of the studies of psychological effects of physical abuse have emphasized the potential for the most dramatic impacts, as in the following characterization: "Like victims of disaster, battered women may experience severe and long-lasting after-effects including shock, numbness, withdrawal, severe depression, and suicidal rumination" (Better Homes Fund, 1994, p. 16; see also Browne, 1987; Walker, 1979). Some observers have suggested that women's response to extreme violence is similar to what is found among concentration camp survivors or victims of torture (Copelon, 1994; Graham, Rawlings, & Rimini, 1988). Most analysts agree that the greatest potential risk of serious psychological harm is found among women who repeatedly experience both physical and sexual assault by a partner (e.g., Dutton, 1992).

Posttraumatic Stress Disorder

Concern about the range of possible psychological effects of battering has spawned significant research on the frequency and conditions under which women develop the most serious combinations of effects that have been described by some people as *battered woman syndrome* (e.g., Douglas, 1987; Walker, 1984, 1991), which has been most recently viewed as a type of posttraumatic stress disorder (PTSD). PTSD was originally conceptualized to explain reactions among survivors of war and natural disasters. It includes psychological and physiological reactions to a traumatic event (or events) that must be present in certain minimum combinations to be applied. The reactions include intrusion (thoughts, nightmares, or memories of the event that appear out of context), avoidance (difficulty remembering, feeling distant or numb), and hyperarousal (such as fear, being extra watchful, outbursts of anger, having trouble sleeping; American Psychiatric Association, 1994).

In general, the evidence collected to date indicates that PTSD symptoms are present in some, but by no means all, battered women. Furthermore, most of the research reported has involved relatively small samples, and much of it has found a relationship between the frequency and severity of abuse and psychological distress; research efforts are still under way to discover the factors that distinguish the battered women who develop these symptoms from those who do not.

Houskamp and Foy (1991) found that 60% of the women who had experienced "high life threat" showed PTSD symptoms, compared to 14% of those who had "low exposure" to threats against their lives. Dutton and Painter (1993), in contrast, found that intermittency and unpredictability of abuse was more strongly associated with PTSD symptoms than were frequency and severity.

Using a somewhat larger sample (179 battered women and 48 verbally abused women), Kemp, Green, Hovanitz, and Rawlings (1995) report that 81% of the physically abused and 63% of verbally abused women met the criteria for PTSD on the measures they used.[1] Furthermore, they found that women who tried to cope with the abuse by using such "disengagement strategies" as wishful thinking, social withdrawal, problem avoidance, and self-criticism had the highest rates of PTSD, whereas those who had more social support had lower levels. Astin, Lawrence, and Foy's (1993) research with 53 battered women receiving shelter or counseling services found that just under half were rated as having PTSD on both of two different measures. The data show that factors that preceded the battering (such as the amount and quality of social support and other life experiences) influenced the intensity of PTSD levels, as did the violence itself.

Research on the presence of PTSD in battered women is still far from definitive. It remains controversial as a way to understand women's behavior (Dutton, 1996b), although specific findings and some applications (as in the defense of battered women accused of attacks on their partners) have been useful in specific cases.

Drug and Alcohol Abuse

Some battered women use drugs or alcohol to cope with the physical and emotional pain of abuse (Miller, Downs, & Gondoli,

1989), and some simply use drugs or alcohol—not as part of any coping strategy (Dutton, 1992). For example, a study that compared women who were incarcerated for killing their partners with women in shelters who had experienced physical abuse over many years found high rates of drug and alcohol use in both groups, but higher rates among the women in prison (Blount, Silverman, Sellers, & Seese, 1994). Sixty-four percent of the women in prison and 44% of the women in shelters reported heavy drinking. In addition, nearly a quarter of the incarcerated women and 8% of the sheltered women said they used marijuana; 10% of the women in prison indicated they were injection drug users. A different study that compared battered women incarcerated for killing or seriously assaulting their partners with battered women incarcerated for other offenses found that the women who killed or assaulted reported significantly less drug use (27% versus 60%, respectively; O'Keefe, 1997). As the inconsistencies in these studies show, there is still much to learn about battered women and substance abuse.

Some researchers have estimated that as much as half of all alcoholism in women may be triggered by abuse (Hotaling & Sugarman, 1986). The national random sample survey found that 13% of the women who reported severe violence in the previous year said their drinking or drug problems had gotten "much worse" during that time (Gelles & Straus, 1988).

Suicide

Research has begun to indicate that battered women are at increased risk for suicide. Studies with shelter and community volunteer samples have found that 35% to 40% of the battered women responding had attempted suicide at least once. A study of 176 women who came to the emergency service at an urban hospital over a 1-year period for attempted suicide found that nearly half of the African American women and 30% of the women overall had been battered (Stark & Flitcraft, 1995).

Child-Related Risks

One of the most significant considerations in most battered women's risk analyses are risks to and involving their children. These considerations might include that an abusive partner is actually hitting or physically hurting the children or that the children are being affected by witnessing the physical violence and other abusive behavior. In addition, when a battered mother factors in staying or leaving a relationship in her risk analysis for her children, she may think about leaving and being on her own, the risks and challenges of single parenting, child care, getting child support, and how she will provide for her children's health care, housing, food, education, and transportation. If an abusive partner has consistently insulted a woman's parenting, she may have doubts about her ability to raise the children by herself. Other concerns may be the effect of a custody battle on the children or growing up in a home without a father—from a "broken family." The mother may worry about whether her children will be safe when they are visiting their father and she is no longer there to intervene on their behalf.

The decision to stay or to leave may place battered mothers in a position in which they are choosing between two negative alternatives. For example, a battered mother may leave an abusive partner because she is worried about her children and child protective services has threatened to remove her children if she does not leave. Unfortunately, her abusive partner, who is not the father of her children, was also her sole source of financial support for herself and her children and now she and her children face homelessness, along with a potential lack of food, clothes, and health care—depending on her ability to find work and child care or her eligibility for minimal and potentially time-limited government benefits.

There is widespread agreement that the direct physical abuse of children can be damaging to them cognitively, emotionally, socially, and in many other ways; that is the principle underlying child protection policies across the country. Several studies have found that in 60% to 75% of the homes where a woman is battered, children are battered as well (Bowker et al., 1988; McKibben, DeVos, & Newberger, 1989). Gelles and Straus (1988) found that in 77% of the families in which women experienced severe violence, the children were abused as well. They also found that half of the men who battered their wives also abused a child more than twice a year. This rate was about seven times the rate found for men who did not abuse their wives (Straus, 1983). In other studies, the percentages of battering men who also abused their children physically ranged from 70% to 40% (e.g., Bowker, Arbitell, & McFarron, 1988; Layzer, Goodson, & deLange, 1986; Suh & Abel, 1990). Clearly, children in homes where their mothers are battered are at higher risk for violence.

Studies of children who "only" witness violence increasingly agree that such exposure can be damaging as well. Child witnesses frequently report being afraid for themselves and their mothers and of uncontrollable changes in their lives. Depending on the frequency and severity of the violence they see, their age and gender, their relationships with the adults in their lives, and other factors, children have been found to experience negative effects in behavioral, emotional, social, cognitive, and physical functioning. (See summaries of this research in Gleason, 1995; Henning, Leitenberg, Coffey, Turner, & Bennett, 1996; Jaffe, Wolfe, & Wilson, 1990; Kolbo, Blakely, & Engleman, 1996; O'Keefe, 1994, 1995; Osofsky, 1995; Peled, 1996.) Such effects have been found to impair school performance and peer relationships and contribute to heightened rates of delinquency in some cases. There is also evidence that boys and girls may be affected differently. One recent study (Kolbo, 1996), for example, found that girls who were exposed to violence in their families were more likely to have behavior problems than girls who were not, and boys who were exposed had lower self-worth. Other studies have found differences, but in the direction of more behavior problems for boys and lower self-worth among girls. There is also evidence that boys who witness violence in childhood are at greater risk of abusing their adult partners (Choice, Lamke, & Pittman, 1995; Gelles & Straus, 1988; Osofsky, 1995). Clearly, although the evidence indicates that children are often affected, much more needs to be learned about the types of effects and the factors involved.

One of the most common threats made by batterers is to take the children away from their mother, either by physically snatching the children or by winning a custody fight. In fact, Liss and Stahly (1993) found that divorce cases in which domestic violence was an issue were more likely than others to include fights over custody. Most battered women weigh this threat heavily in their risk analysis. If a battered woman is trying to leave the relationship, she may be concerned for her children's safety if their father is physically abusive or neglectful to them and he will have visitation that will expose the children to this danger. In addition, some battered women weigh the possibility of losing their children to child protective services if they are accused of endangering their children's safety. For many women, the abuse of their children is the "final straw" that leads them to take more vigorous action to enhance their safety. Gelles and Straus (1988), for example, report that "many women left immediately after their teenage children had been hurt trying to protect them" (p. 144). There is substantial anecdotal evidence that this is a common pattern. Kurz (1996) reports that of the divorced women in her study who left the relationship because of violence, one of the two major reasons was that "they believed that seeing the violence was harming their children's emotional well-being" (p. 68). Similarly, Henderson (1990) reports that women were concerned about the developmental effect on their children of growing up in a home where their mother was abused; they did not want the children to learn "to accept it" (p. 11).

In her study of 129 divorced mothers, Kurz (1995) asked if the women were ever afraid for themselves or their children during custody negotiations; 38% said they were. The interviews provide numerous examples of the men threatening to take the children and keep custody of them, often as a strategy to obtain something else they wanted. For example:

> He wanted custody. It was a long heated matter. He'd say I was an unfit mother. . . . I said I was going to get my own lawyer, then he would back down. He threatened to take my son off me. Sometimes I thought he would take him and not bring him back. (p. 159)

Another woman stated, "At one point my husband threatened me by saying, 'if you don't give me such-and-such I'll take the children.' I had my lawyer call him and tell him if he didn't stop it he'd have him sent to jail" (p. 159). Some of the women in this study reported that they had reduced their demands for child support and other resources because of their fears of losing custody.

Financial Risks

Money is among the most important aspects of risk analysis. Battered women come from all socioeconomic classes and their financial considerations are as diverse as they are.

For some battered women, financial security may mean just having the basics—food, shelter, clothes, health care. For some poor women, this might mean living anywhere they can afford, even if it includes substandard conditions, surviving on food stamps and donated clothes, and going to the emergency clinic when the children need medical attention. For other women, financial security might mean safe, quality child care, living where they want to live, in a house where the neighborhood is safe and the schools are good. It may mean having a job that pays well and is fulfilling and provides flexibility for child rearing, belonging to a certain social class or group, having a comfortable retirement, having the opportunity to travel, going on family vacations, having new cars, sending the children to private schools or college, and buying them sporting equipment, music lessons, and so on. Most batterers are skilled at controlling their partners by threatening their financial security and independence. The fact that many battered women are either fully or partially dependent on their partner's income for support of themselves and their children adds to the power of the threat.

If a woman stays in a relationship, her partner may control all the money. He may give her a certain amount of money to buy food and household necessities and she may have to account to him for every dollar. He might stop paying the rent or mortgage and threaten to leave her and the children without a home. She may face eviction because of his damage to her apartment or because she has repeatedly called the police and the neighbors have complained to the landlord. A batterer may keep his partner from working, from working in a "good" job, or from going to school or training to increase her job opportunities.

On the other hand, if a woman leaves the relationship, she and her children may face a significant decrease in their standard of living. She may have to move to a more affordable neighborhood, go from living in a house to an apartment, leave a good job, move the children to a new school, lose her present child care. She may be unable to afford things for the children, such as going to movies and buying sneakers, clothes, lessons, toys, and computers. She may lose a support system such as family, friends, neighbors, religious community, and social services. If she is forced to give up her housing completely and go into temporary shelter or onto the streets, both she and her children could face many risks. If she becomes homeless, her children could be removed by child protective services. A battered woman may face the uncertainty of trying to survive on government benefits and suffer the stigma and blame placed on such recipients.

Although there is anecdotal evidence of the direct financial risks battered women face because of abuse, researchers are just beginning to investigate this issue systematically. One such effort was a study in New York City that found that 56% of working battered women had lost a job because of violence and 75% had their employment jeopardized by the frequent harassment they experienced from their partners while they were at work (Friedman & Couper, 1987).

This issue is a central one for women. Research that has looked at the factors that distinguish the women who left their abusive partner and stayed away from those who returned has often found that employment was one important consideration. For example, I. Johnson's (1992) study of 426 women who sought shelter services found that family income, the woman's employment, the severity of the abuse, and the woman's self-conception were the major factors that distinguished the two groups. Johnson found, however, that it was not the amount of family income that explained the difference in the two groups, but whether or not the woman was able to control some of the money coming into the household. When women were employed and able to control that income, they were less likely to stay with their abusive partners.

If women have no independent source of income, homelessness may be their primary option to remaining with their abuser. As more research has been conducted with people who are homeless, it has become apparent that domestic violence is a major contributor to homelessness among women (Bassuk & Rosenberg, 1988; Better Homes Fund, 1994).

Risks to Family and Friends

Concerns about family and friends significantly influence some battered women's risk analyses. The two major concerns women have are the potential for losing the support of family and friends and the fear that the family and friends may be physically injured and/or threatened. Whether women stay in or leave a relationship, they may lose contact and support from family or friends. A woman's abusive partner may prevent her from having contact or may try to turn the woman's family and friends against her. If family or friends try to intervene, a batterer may turn his violence toward them.

Family and friends are often one of the greatest resources for women in abusive relationships, providing emotional and financial support, a place to stay, a shoulder to cry on, or help with the children. Bowker (1983) found that friends were the most common source of informal help that battered women relied on. Gelles and Straus (1988) found that informal sources of help were the ones women were most likely to use. The studies of PTSD symptoms (Dutton & Painter, 1993; Houskamp & Foy, 1991) found that social support from friends and family was among the factors most commonly associated with lower levels of symptoms.

Friends and family may be unwilling to serve as a source of support indefinitely, however, especially if they feel that the woman should take steps she is not prepared to take. Listening to stories of abuse can be a difficult experience over time. Davis, Hagen, and Early (1994) found that the rape and assault of women had negative psychological consequences for their friends and family—particularly for their female associates. The impact of ongoing abuse on these relationships can be prominent considerations for battered women. Over time, they may become ashamed that the abuse continues, and begin to cut themselves off out of embarrassment. Their shame at not taking the actions their friends advise, coupled with possible recurring visible evidence of on- going abuse, can contribute to their isolating themselves from outside social support.

More commonly, batterers may keep their partners isolated from family and friends to cut off such forms of support. Kelly (1996) notes that "jealous surveillance" by batterers can lead to the destruction of other relationships. Other batterers threaten family or friends who try to help their partners. If a woman goes into hiding, her abusive partner may try to find out where she is by asking or threatening family and friends.

Rosemary

Rosemary and John grew up together and have been married for 3 years. Their families are close friends and they all live in the same small rural town. John works with Rosemary's brother and father in the family-owned business. Rosemary works as a paralegal in a local law firm, and her mother provides day care for their only child. John is very possessive and extremely jealous of the men Rosemary meets at work. He dictates what Rosemary can wear to work and calls her several times during the day. John drives her to work and picks her up at the office. Last week, when John picked her up, Rosemary was walking out the door at the same time one of the male attorneys was leaving. John yelled at her to get in the car and sped off. When they got home, he tore her clothes and accused her of sleeping with the attorney and called her a whore. He shoved her around, knocked her on the floor, and kicked her. He said she had to quit or he was going to get her fired. Rosemary wants to keep her job and is confused about John's behavior because it is the first time he has ever hit her. Rosemary talks to her family and her mother-in-law, but is concerned that they blame her for her marriage problems. Her family is angry at John and want to fire him from the family business. They remind her that they never approved of her marriage to John, and her brother tells her he is going to have a talk with

John "to straighten him out." Her mother-in-law tells her that all young couples go through this. She suggests John won't be jealous anymore if Rosemary quits work and has another baby.

Rosemary's Risk Analysis. The risks in Rosemary's analysis incorporate John's behavior toward her, including his extreme jealousy and physical violence against her and her concern that she will lose her job if John carries out his threat to get her fired. Yet Rosemary's risk analysis is also intertwined with her relationship with her family and her in-laws. When this additional layer of considerations is added, additional risks arise in her analysis, including John's losing his job because her family fires him. The more she tells them about John, the greater the chance that this risk may be realized. She is also concerned she cannot talk to her family about John at all.

- She is worried about losing her family's support completely. They want her to leave John and she's worried that if she does not, they may not be there for her anymore.
- She is worried about her brother or John getting hurt. She is not sure how John will react to her brother confronting him. She is very concerned that if John finds out she talked to her family, he will be angry and maybe hurt her again. She also knows her brother can lose his temper and is worried he and John will fight and hurt each other.
- She is worried that if she tries to leave John, it will damage the friendly relationship between the families, and some friends in the small town would take sides.
- She is worried about alienating her in-laws. They have been very understanding and supportive of her and John. Rosemary is concerned that if she does not quit her job, John's family may blame her for causing the marriage to fail. She does not want to lose their support because she believes they can help her change John.
- She may lose her alternate day care arrangement. Sometimes her mother-in-law watches their child while she works, and she is worried John will tell his mother to stop providing day care.

Loss of Relationship

For many women, having an adult intimate relationship is an essential part of life. Such relationships can provide companionship and a sense of family and home. For some women, a relationship provides a definition of who they are and an opportunity to fulfill a particular role. Women may feel a sense of loyalty to their partners and a responsibility to make the relationship work. Some battered women love their partners. Love for a partner and commitment to a relationship can be powerful aspects of a woman's risk analysis. Studies have found that battered women often continue to love their partners, at least following the initial acts of violence. Barnett and Lopez-Real (1985; cited in Barnett & LaViolette, 1993) found that the single most common reason battered women gave for staying in their relationship was their hope that their partner would change; love for their partner was tied with lack of monetary resources or job training as the third most common reason.

For some women, the risk of losing their relationship is more about the fear of being alone than about losing their partner's love. They may believe they cannot survive alone and fear that horrible things might happen to them without their partner's presence. A fear of being alone can be exacerbated if a woman has never been on her own before. It can also be exacerbated by a concern that she will not be able to find another relationship. If a battered woman thinks about leaving permanently, she must analyze the effect of losing her relationship. Yet, even if she stays, a battered woman may lose her partner. Her partner may decide to leave. This, too, will be part of her risk analysis about her relationship.

Physical and emotional violence is one of the major reasons women end or lose relationships. The research literature on divorce, when this issue is explored, demonstrates that violence is a primary contributor to divorce. For example, Ellis and Stuckless studied 362 separating husbands and wives. They report that more than 40% of the wives said that they were injured by their partners at some time during the relationship, and 57% said abuse by their partner was a major reason for separating (cited in Kurz, 1996, p. 67). Ellis and DeKeseredy (1989) found that over half of the separating women in their study reported that abuse was one of the reasons they decided to separate.

Not all the women who divorce or separate and have experienced violence during their relationship claim that was the main reason for ending the relationship, however. For example, Kurz's (1995) study of 129 divorced mothers found that 70% had experienced violence during their marriage. Of this group, however, just 19% said they left the marriage because of the violence.

Risks Involving Arrest and Legal Status

For some women, arrest or their residency or citizenship status will be part of their risk analyses. A batterer may coerce his partner to participate in criminal activity or she may be implicated in his criminal activity. He might also use the threat of "turning her in" to control her and keep her from leaving. If a woman has to defend herself or her children from her partner's physical violence, she could be arrested and prosecuted for that action. This might be a particular fear for a woman who has called the police in the past and their response was to arrest her or both her and her partner. Saunders's (1995) study of police officers' inclination to arrest a victim who had called them found that 15% said there was a "good likelihood" that they would arrest the woman who called in addition to her abuser. Those who said they would be likely to arrest the victim were also more likely to find domestic violence justified under some circumstances and to be more uncomfortable talking with victims. Saunders speculates that the tendency to arrest might be stronger if mandatory arrest were in effect. In addition, arrest of an abusive partner might be a risk for a woman, particularly if the arrest will lead to other risks such as retribution, loss of his job and income, or public embarrassment. Several studies of mandatory arrest have found that women who have called the police during an attack by their abusive partner have been arrested as well because of their partner's counterclaims (e.g., Lyon & Mace, 1991).

Richie's (1996) study of battered women who were incarcerated provides widely varied examples of these fears and considerations becoming reality. The women Richie interviewed had been coerced or manipulated into criminal activity, had been threatened with arrest by their partners (who had ultimately followed through on the threats), and had become involved in illegal drug use to numb the pain of their abuse.

For battered women whose residency status depends on their partner or for undocumented battered women, the risk of losing their status or being turned into the Immigration and Naturalization Service is a significant aspect of their risk analysis (Jang, 1994; Orloff, Jang, & Klein, 1995).

Leaving a relationship will not necessarily alleviate these risks for a battered woman and may motivate her partner to carry out his threats. For example, a woman may still have to defend herself after she has left. In addition, leaving a relationship could increase a battered woman's chances of losing residency status, despite recent legal changes mandated by the Violence Against Women Act of 1994. Some batterers will keep their partners from having accurate information about immigration or residency issues, and battered women may rely solely on their partners for such information due to language and other barriers.

Implications for Advocacy

Elements of Woman-Defined Advocacy

1. Understand a battered woman's perspective, including her risk analysis and safety plan.
   - Understand a battered woman's risk analysis.
     - Identify the range of batterer-generated risks in a woman's analysis.
     - Identify the effect of staying or leaving on those risks.

Understanding battered women's risk analyses, like understanding any aspect of their perspectives, begins with gathering information. Getting that information requires basic listening skills and a genuine respect for the life, culture, and decision making of each individual battered woman.

How to Gather Information

Gathering information from battered women involves approaching each woman as an individual with different issues, realities, information, and options; remaining sensitive to how she may be experiencing the interaction; using basic listening skills; and respecting the woman and what she has to say. There are three key aspects to gathering information: approaching each battered woman as a unique individual, listening effectively, and understanding that a woman's perspective will change.

Each Battered Woman Is an Individual

All battered women have in common a partner or ex-partner who uses whatever strategies are necessary to control them or some aspect of their lives. How each woman experiences that control, how she responds, what she fears, what options are available to her, what options she perceives to be available to her, and how the people she encounters will respond to her are unique to each woman. Understanding this uniqueness is essential for woman-defined advocacy. Therefore, each woman's "story" must be heard each time an advocate seeks to help. In addition, hearing each woman's unique story can help to avoid assumptions or judgments that can originate from class, race, or cultural biases or ignorance.

When an advocate talks with battered women, each woman will be at a different point in her life with a particular experience of the battering. The advocate may be talking with her as she is being attacked, shortly after, or weeks or months later. Alternatively, the advocate may talk with a woman whose partner has just threatened to snatch the children. In addition, each woman is juggling other life concerns while she interacts with an advocate. She may be on her way to work, worrying about who will pick up her children from the school bus, getting ready for her sister's wedding, or studying for final exams. An interaction with an advocate is only one of the things a battered woman is handling. An awareness that each battered woman may have other things on her mind, and that these things will be different for each woman, will help the advocacy be woman defined.

Listen Effectively

Listening is a common and familiar advocacy skill. As advocates know, listening involves much more than just hearing the words a woman is speaking. It means putting yourself in her shoes, under-standing her life and how she views and experiences the violence in it. It means understanding and accepting unfamiliar views, beliefs, and cultures. Advocates can do a number of things to ensure that they truly listen.

Create a Safe Place. On a practical level, trying to create a safe place to talk can be important. If the conversation is over the phone, then telecommunications privacy issues such as "caller identification" should be addressed.[2] If the conversation is in person, then it may help to pay attention to the physical surroundings. Advocates might ask themselves:

- Is the place physically safe? Can anyone walk in at any time? If a battered woman and her partner are in court, the doctor's office, or some other location at the same time, could the woman's partner find her and threaten her? Are there sheriffs, guards, security staff around that understand the potential danger and can respond?
- What does it feel like to be here? Is it loud, with many distractions? What is hanging on the wall? How would various battered women view it? For example, many women with violent partners do not consider themselves battered or abused, so posters about domestic violence and battering may be ineffective or make women feel the advocate will not be able to help them.

- Is it private? Can others hear what you are saying or see if a woman is afraid, angry, crying, or upset? Privacy may encourage women to talk, particularly with the range of very personal matters necessary for effective safety planning.
- How is written information handled? Can a woman see other women's files or papers lying around the office or desk? How might she perceive this?

Often privacy—meaning a third party cannot overhear a conversation or see written information—is a requirement for confidential or privileged communications legal protection to be enforced. The law assumes that if other people can hear or see the information, then the woman did not intend for it to be kept confidential, and therefore the court and/or the woman's partner has a right to find out what it is. Because effective woman-defined advocacy relies on complete information, confidentiality is essential. Every effort must be made to protect the privacy of battered women.

It is not always possible to provide the best surroundings to talk with women. Limited agency budgets mean cramped and less-than-ideal surroundings. Yet many changes can be made with little expense, such as ensuring that files and information are kept securely. Even if limited resources preclude improvements, it is important to at least be aware of the effect of surroundings on women.

Start With Her Concerns, Her Questions, What She Wants to Tell You. Starting with the woman's concerns or questions—her story—sets the tone for the rest of the conversation. It can build trust, show respect, and provide the framework for the rest of the interaction. Women often begin with their greatest concern or what they think the advocate can help them with. When the advocate starts with the woman's concerns and questions, the advocate does not waste time talking about irrelevant issues, services, or information. Experience with woman-defined advocacy has shown that starting with the woman's perspective first can save time. The amount of time available for advocacy can have a significant effect on advocacy. Advocates often do not have a lot of time to talk with women. Sometimes this leads advocates to do all the talking. For example, advocates may say, "I only have 15 minutes, so I make sure I describe all the services so she'll know about them." This approach does provide information about services. It does not explore if the services are, or ever will be, relevant to a particular woman. Most important, when the advocate does most of the talking, she does not establish a relationship or trust with the woman. Without such a relationship or trust, it is less likely the woman will contact the advocate again. Because in many situations the advocate is the access to other services and provides essential information and support, this approach could limit an advocate's ability to help women.

Communicate simply and effectively. Sometimes, something as simple as starting with open-ended questions can help an advocate start with the woman's perspective. Examples of these types of questions are: How can I help you? What made you pick up the phone and call us? What made you call the police last night? What do you want to see happen? What are your biggest concerns right now? What are you worried about? How are your children dealing with this?

Another simple, yet often neglected, technique for building a woman's confidence in herself and trust in the advocate is validating what the woman is saying and showing respect her for life, differences, and perspective. Validation might include using some of the following phrases:

- You're doing well.
- You're handling so much.
- You've made a lot of plans—that's good.
- You really care about your kids.
- I admire your strength to deal with all you're dealing with.
- I understand why you'd want to [fill in the blank].
- What you're trying to do is really hard and you've done a lot already [and then list for her the strategies she's used].
- Your family seems to really care about you.
- Your children are really connected to you.

It is also important to clarify what the advocate does not understand. Advocates may have expertise on general domestic violence issues or a particular service system, but they cannot be experts on each individual woman's life—only the woman can. This is particularly important to keep in mind if the woman and the advocate are from different cultures or backgrounds. If something the woman says does not make sense to the advocate or the advocate sees it differently, the advocate must find out why. Sometimes the confusion is simply because the advocate needs more or different information and sometimes it is a miscommunication or misunderstanding based on cultural differences.

Because so much of advocacy is getting and giving information, it is crucial to say things in a way women will understand. Language barriers can limit an advocate's ability to communicate with a battered woman. This means that the advocate should use the woman's primary language. Because advocates may not speak that language, providing and communicating effectively with an interpreter is another listening skill. It is important for an advocate to recognize when a language barrier is having a negative effect on the working relationship with a woman or the amount and quality of information she is getting. An advocate may be able to gather a general sense of the woman's situation, but probably will not have all the significant details or nuances of a woman's fears or strategies. Advocates may need to develop new skills to gather information through an interpreter. For example, a good practice when working with an interpreter is for the advocate to place herself so she is talking and looking at the battered woman, not the interpreter.

The use of jargon can get in the way of gathering information, giving information, and building trust. Advocates have their own jargon, such as "shelter," "crisis intervention," "safety plans," "hotline," "cycle of violence," "batterer," and "secondary victims." Advocates often work within or with systems that have additional jargon. For example, the legal system's jargon includes "probable cause," "protective order," "plaintiff," and "mandatory reporter." Jargon may save time when speaking to others who know and use it, and it may add to an advocate's credibility and effectiveness when he or she works within particular systems. When advocates use jargon with battered women, however, they may be communicating ineffectively—wasting time and potentially misleading women. Jargon can also set up a counterproductive power dynamic—the advocate with the information and the power and the woman without. Advocates should try to recognize when they hear and use jargon and find new, simple ways of explaining what they are trying to convey.

Be Aware of the Woman's Assessment of the Advocate. As the advocate communicates with a battered woman, the battered woman is assessing the interaction and the advocate. She may assess the advocate's sensitivity, understanding, and ability to help. Sometimes an interaction can get off on the wrong foot. If the advocate knows when this is happening, he or she can usually fix it. Often, simply reaffirming concern for the woman, refocusing on the woman's concerns, and checking for any miscommunication can make the interaction more positive.

Understand That a
Woman's Perspective Will Change

Each battered woman has a unique perspective and each woman's perspective, risk analysis, and safety plans will change. A woman's hopes and fears for her relationship, her children, and her life ebb and flow as she tries new strategies to improve things or just keep things quiet. Often a woman's hope that her partner will change rises when a system, particularly the legal system, intervenes; "he's finally going to get the help he needs" or "someone is finally going to punish him for what he's done to me." All too often, these hopes are not realized and the hope and fear balance shifts again. The woman's strategies change and her risk analysis and safety plans will be refined to include what she has learned and how her partner reacts. These changes often reflect accurate assessments of her risks and options.

Changing risk analyses and plans will have a significant effect on advocacy. For example, if a woman's risk analysis shifts from seeing physical violence as the greatest risk and leaving as the best strategy to child protective services' involvement and losing her children as the greatest risk and staying as the best strategy, then advocacy with this woman will also need to shift. Advocates should anticipate that there will be changes. They should also remain open to new and different information, risk analyses, and plans each time they talk with the woman.

What Information to Gather
About Batterer-Generated Risks

- Discover the range of batterer-generated risks the woman is thinking about.
- Do not limit the inquiry to physical violence.
- Consider asking additional questions such as, What things are you worried about right now? We've talked about [fill in the blank]. Are there other things you're concerned about?
- Find out the woman's perspective on the effect staying or leaving may have on the risks she has identified. Consider asking the following kinds of questions:
- If you stay with your partner, do you think that would make things better or worse for you? How?

- If you left or tried to leave do you think that would make things better or worse for you? How?

Karen

Karen and Don have been married for 7 years. They have two children, Vivian, 6, and Zack, 2. Don works as a machine operator and Karen works part time as a secretary. They own a home with a big mortgage. Don's mother watches Zack when Karen works. Don frequently goes out with his friends, leaving Karen home alone with the children. Last year, she tried to talk with him about it and they got into a big fight. He punched her in the face and choked her. He didn't come home for 3 days. The children got scared that they had lost their father, and recently Vivian has started to have trouble in school. Since then, Karen made up her mind to just keep quiet, even though she thinks he may be having an affair. He hasn't hit her since, but tells her, "Just remember who's in charge here, bitch—mind your own business or else."

Karen's risk analysis. At first glance, an advocate might assume that Karen's risk analysis would include the following risks:

- Physical violence and threats from Don
- How the children are doing in school
- Don having an affair

Further discussion with Karen would uncover additional risks:

- Karen is worried that she may be losing her mind. She feels like she cannot do anything right, that she is always "walking on eggshells," never knowing what he will do. She has been having trouble concentrating at work and cannot seem to get a good night's sleep.
- She is worried her kids are doing poorly in school because she is a bad mother.
- She is worried about Don having sex with other people. He sometimes forces her to do things that hurt her and she is worried she might get AIDS or some other disease.

- Karen really likes her job and she is afraid that Don may force her to quit or make her lose her job. She has stopped after work to have a drink with one of her coworkers a couple of times and she is afraid Don will find out.

As Karen adds the consideration of leaving Don to her analysis, additional risks and considerations arise:

- How will Don react? One time she brought up the topic of divorce and he got very angry and slapped her so hard he split her lip. She is worried that he may get more violent if she tries to leave.
- Karen is worried about her kids having to go through a divorce. Don may try to get custody.
- Karen is analyzing the financial risks if she leaves. She is not sure she could get Don to move out of the house, and even if he did, she is not sure how she would pay the mortgage. She knows she would not get that much child support and that Don would probably figure out a way to stop paying. Her part-time job does not pay enough to live on. Vivian has asthma, and the medication is expensive. Karen is thinking about whether Don will keep up the health insurance he gets through work.
- Don's mother has been a good source of support to her and Karen is worried that if she tries to leave, her mother-in-law will take his side and stop watching Zack while she works, and she will lose her friendship as well.
- Karen is also afraid of being alone. Karen left her parents' house when she married Don, so she has never lived alone. She is sure she will never find someone else and just does not think she can make it on her own.

As this example illustrates, a battered woman's risk analysis is complex and will change when women consider the possibility of leaving the relationship. Additional changes will occur as women explore the resources and options available to them. These are discussed in Chapter 5, "Battered Women's Decision Making and Safety Plans."

Conclusion

Battered women analyze the risks to themselves and their children on an ongoing basis. One day a woman may believe that her greatest risk is losing her home; the next day she may believe her greatest risk is that she will be killed. For some battered women, the decision to leave will increase the severity and number of risks they face. For others, leaving will lessen the risks.

Figure 3.1 was developed to compare some of the risks that women may face in their relationships and to explore what effect staying in or leaving these relationships may have on those risks. Some women may face a few of these risks, whereas other women may experience most or all of these risks. Figure 3.1 summarizes the two key points of this chapter. First, battered women's risk analyses include a consideration of more risks than physical violence. Second, women's lives are not necessarily made better or safer by leaving the relationship. That is not to say that women should stay in violent relationships, but rather to acknowledge the reality that the options and choices available to women who want to leave are often limited or nonexistent.

Notes

1. Kemp et al. (1995) note the limitations of the study in its use of a "convenience" sample of women from shelters and the community. They also raise questions about the diagnosis measures:

> Finding a relationship between verbal abuse and PTSD poses an issue for the present version of the diagnosis. According to the DSM-III-R, the first requirement is the presence of trauma that requires a physical threat to one's life or physical integrity, to family, to home, or the witnessing of violence. Verbal abuse does not fit in these categories. (p. 53)

2. If a person purchases a caller identification service and has the equipment to display incoming numbers, then the phone number of an unblocked incoming call will be displayed, even if the call was not answered. Some equipment also records a list of phone numbers. In some areas, a person making a call can block the number from being identified by having a special line-blocking feature or by dialing *67 before dialing the number one is calling.

Possible Risks if She Stays in the Relationship	Possible Risks if She Leaves the Relationship
Physical	
Physical injury: He can continue to hit her and injure her.	Physical injury: He may continue to hit and injure her. Some studies have shown he may be more likely to hurt her after she has left.
Death: He may kill her.	Death: Threats can surface when a woman explores leaving or tries to leave, "If I can't have you nobody will." Leaving does not ensure that he will not find her and may increase the chance she will be killed.
HIV: Through unsafe behavior with her partner, she may have no choice regarding sex, including whether to practice safer sex; he may sexually assault her.	HIV: Unsafe behavior with her partner may continue; he may sexually assault her.
Much advocacy ends at this point on this list of risks that women with violent partners face. The risks that follow are acknowledged, and advocates do try to respond to these concerns. The primary resources, options and services are designed to address physical risks, however.	
Psychological	
Psychological harm: His use of violence to keep control will continue to affect her and he can continue to attack her verbally and emotionally.	Psychological harm: He may continue to have access to her, particularly if they have children in common and there is ongoing contact due to court-ordered visitation.
Substance abuse: She may abuse drugs and/or alcohol to help her cope with the emotional and physical pain.	Substance abuse: Even if she leaves, she will take an addiction with her; she may abuse drugs and/or alcohol to cope with her new life situation.
Long-term effects: She may experience long-term psychological issues.	Long-term effects: She may experience long-term psychological issues.
Suicide (victim, partner): He could commit murder/suicide; she may commit suicide as a result of the psychological effects of his violence or her desire to take control of a death she may believe is inevitable.	Suicide (victim, partner): He could commit murder/suicide; she may commit suicide as a result of the psychological effects of his violence or her desire to take control of a death she may believe is inevitable.

Figure 3.1. Battered Women's Analysis: Batterer-Generated Risks
SOURCE: © Greater Hartford Legal Assistance, Inc. Used with permission.

Possible Risks if She Stays in the Relationship	Possible Risks if She Leaves the Relationship
Children	
Physical injury or psychological harm to children: Children can witness violence, be the object of physical violence or psychological attack, be hurt while trying to protect their mother.	Physical injury or psychological harm to children: Children can witness violence, be the object of physical violence or psychological attack, be hurt while trying to protect their mother, may be at greater risk while on visitation without parent-victim present; no visitation may also harm the child.
Loss of children: Child protective services could become involved if violence is disclosed, "failure to protect"-type arguments could be used to place children in foster care or proceed on termination of parental rights case.	Loss of children: He could legally gain custody or just take the children; child protective services could still be involved or become involved.
Being alone, single parenting: He could be emotionally unavailable; he could do little to help her with the children.	Being alone, single parenting: He is unavailable, and she may not be able (or want) to "find someone new"; he may not visit or help raise the children; it may not be safe for the children or her to have him do so.
Financial	
Standard of living: He may control the money and give her little money to live on; he could lose or quit his job; he could make her lose or quit her job.	Standard of living: She may now live solely on her income; she may have to move out of her home, neighborhood; she may have less money; he could make her lose her job.
Loss of income/job: He could keep her from working, limit how much she works; he may sabotage her efforts to find a job, succeed at a job, or pursue job training.	Loss of income/job: She could lose his income, have to quit a job to relocate, have to quit if she has become a single parent; he could keep her from working by harassment, threats.
Loss of housing: She could be evicted due to "disturbance" or damage he has done.	Loss of housing: She may need to move out to leave the relationship or go into hiding for safety; she could lose her residence as part of a divorce.
Loss or damage to possessions: He may destroy things of importance or value to her to further his control.	Loss or damage to possessions: He may destroy things of importance or value to her to further his control; she may have to leave things behind when she leaves; he may win the right to possessions in a divorce roceeding.
	(continued)

Figure 3.1. Continued

Possible Risks if She Stays in the Relationship	Possible Risks if She Leaves the Relationship
Family and Friends	
Threat or injury to family or friends: Family and friends may be at risk, particularly if they try to intervene.	Threat or injury to family or friends: Friends or family may be at risk, particularly if they try to intervene, protect the woman, provide her with housing; threat can be used to keep a woman from going into hiding—"If I don't know where you are I'll get your family."
Loss of family or friends' support: They may want her to leave and stop supporting her if she stays; they may not like him or may be afraid of him; he may keep her isolated from them.	Loss of family or friends' support: They may not want her to leave him; they may blame her for the end of the relationship.
Relationship	
Loss of partner or relationship: He could leave her or be unavailable emotionally.	Loss of partner or relationship: Leaving means the loss of her partner and significant change to the relationship.
Loss of caretaker: If she is disabled and he is her caretaker, he may not adequately care for her.	Loss of caretaker: If she is disabled and he is her caretaker, he will no longer be there to help her
Arrest, Legal Status	
Her arrest: He could threaten to turn her in or turn her in if she has participated in criminal activity; he may threaten this to keep her from leaving; he may force her to participate in criminal activity; she may defend herself against him and be charged with a crime. Arrest could lead to incarceration, loss of job, loss of children, public embarrassment, etc.	Her arrest: He could threaten to turn her in or turn her in if she has participated in criminal activity; he may force her to be involved in criminal activity; she may defend herself against him and be charged with a crime. Arrest could lead to incarceration, loss of job, loss of children, public embarrassment, etc.
Partner's arrest: He might be arrested leading to his retaliation, the loss of his job, public embarrassment for her and her family.	Partner's arrest: He might be arrested leading to his retaliation, the loss of his job, public embarrassment for her and her family.
Loss of residency status: He could carry out that threat.	Loss of residency status: He could carry out that threat.

Figure 3.1. Continued

4

Life-Generated Risks

Not all the risks a battered woman includes in her risk analysis are batterer-generated. *Life-generated risks* and circumstances, such as financial limitations and racism and other biases, are aspects of women's lives over which they may have little or no control. These types of risks are also sometimes called environmental or social risks. If a woman is aware of life-generated risks, she will consider them in her analysis and planning. If not, the woman may consider the risk only once it actually affects her present plans. The woman may also consider how her abusive partner uses life-generated risks to further his control. This chapter explores only a few of the many life-generated considerations: financial, home location, physical and mental health, inadequate responses by major social institutions, and discrimination based on race, ethnicity, gender, sexual orientation, or other bias. These areas are used as examples of life-generated risks, and therefore the discussion is limited to a brief description of each of these large and complex topics.

Financial Considerations

A battered woman's financial risks and considerations may have nothing to do with her batterer's behavior. For example, she or her partner may be laid off because of corporate downsizing. Although the layoff is not batterer generated, she will have to consider this loss of income, and perhaps health insurance or other benefits, in her analysis and safety plans. A woman who has lost her job may need to wait until she has a new one before she can leave the relationship, or a woman who is laid off while she is trying to save enough money to leave her relationship may have to delay her plans.

In addition, a life-generated risk may increase or add batterer-generated risks, such as a batterer who gets more violent when he is unemployed. A batterer may also use a financial situation to further his control. For example, he may tell his partner that they cannot afford to have a telephone to isolate her further and prevent her from calling the police.

A battered woman's economic opportunities may be limited by lack of child care, transportation, access to training or education, limited available jobs, and the fact that women earn less than men in a majority of occupations (Seavey, 1996). In 1995, married women had higher rates of unemployment than men did, and the gap between married men and women had grown over the previous year (*Employment and Earnings*, 1997). Furthermore, not all the women were working as much as they wanted. Twenty-seven percent of all employed women worked part time in 1996—only partly by choice. Part time workers are much less likely to receive health and other benefits. Further, they earned just over a third of the income received by women employed full time.

In 1996, the median employment-related income from all jobs combined for women who worked full time was just 75% of men's earnings, and had dropped from 76% in 1994 (*Employment and Earnings*, 1997). The gap between women's and men's wages and salaries varied widely—from 85% for public school teachers, nearly 90% for service workers, and 82% for waitresses compared to waiters, to 67% for retail sales people, 69% for managers and administrators, and 60% for people in all types of sales work combined. These are among the most popular types of jobs for women, and some of them are not well paid even compared to those of other working women. For example, women who worked in retail sales had median earnings that were just 62% of the median for all full-time employed women, and women made up 62% of all the people who worked in retail sales full time (*Employment and Earnings*, 1997).[1] Faced with these potential income realities, women have good reason to pause before assuming full independent economic responsibility for themselves and their children.

These economic realities will be incorporated into a battered woman's risk analysis. She may ask herself, How will I support myself and my children? Will I be able to find work? Will the job have health benefits? Will I be able to find affordable, quality child care? How will

I get to work? Will I find affordable housing? How will I get the training or education I need to get ahead? If I cannot find work and day care, will I be able to receive government benefits? How long will they be available? A batterer may use his partner's doubts about her financial security to reinforce the message that she will not be able to make it without him.

When women are unable to develop the economic and other resources to support themselves and their children, yet decide they must leave their abusing partner anyway, they often must face the prospect of living without consistent, reliable shelter. Women represent the fastest growing group of poor and homeless people, most often women on their own with one or two children (Bassuk, 1991). In some studies, homeless women report that abuse by an intimate was one of the primary reasons they left their prior housing and found themselves with no alternative to homelessness (e.g., Hagen, 1987). For example, D'Ercole and Struening (1990) found that 63% of the homeless women in their sample had been battered. In other studies that compared homeless women with poor women who had housing, most found that the experience of adult physical abuse was higher among the homeless women. Bassuk and Rosenberg (1988) found comparative rates of 41% and 20%, respectively, whereas 34% and 16% of Wood, Valdez, Hayashi, and Shin's (1990) respondents reported abuse by their partner. One study of mothers who received Aid to Families with Dependent Children (AFDC) found that 64% of the homeless women and 70% of those who had housing had been physically abused by their partners (Goodman, 1991). Finally, a recent comparative study of homeless and housed mothers in a mid-sized Massachusetts city found that more than 63% of the homeless and 58% of the housed mothers had experienced "severe physical violence" by an intimate partner during adulthood; nearly a third reported such violence within the past two years (Bassuk et al., 1996). These are certainly high rates of abuse; they reflect the complexity of poor and battered women's experiences.

For women with few or no financial resources, the limitations and conditions for receiving government benefits and subsidies may be part of their analysis. Government benefits might include a number of state and federal programs such as cash assistance programs, subsidized housing programs, food stamps, supplemental security income, social security, disability, job training, education, medical benefits, child care, and transportation to work or educational opportunities.

The Personal Responsibility and Work Opportunity Reconciliation Act of 1996 ensures that state and federal benefits programs will continue to be in a constant process of change and funding uncertainty. What benefits will be available, who will be eligible, for how long and for how much, what work requirements will exist, and how the benefits will be paid are all in a state of flux. Particular benefits may no longer exist or may become time limited. This is already the reality in some states. The uncertainties involved make effective safety planning more difficult. Without assurances of jobs that pay a living wage and safety and other supports battered women need, time restrictions, work requirements, and other conditions established by the act will increase the life-generated risks low-income battered women and children face (Davies, 1997).

Home Location

Where women live with their abusive partners can be another source of life-generated risk. For example, more resources tend to be available in cities, yet they may be concentrated in particular areas. Making use of support services may be complicated by the limits and safety of public transportation. Similarly, the higher crime rates common to large urban areas may mean that friends, family, or formal support alternatives such as social service agencies or police take the violence less seriously. Furthermore, although women may hope that they can "get lost in the crowd" of a large city if they want to, they may also be concerned about their partner's network of acquaintances seeing and reporting on their whereabouts.

Contrary to popular images of violence concentrated in cities, limited but growing evidence indicates that women who live in rural areas are not immune from violence, and can also experience heightened risks due to their location and the culture that commonly accompanies living in small country communities. Service alternatives, for example, are typically more limited in rural areas, as is public transportation. In his research on battered women in Kentucky, Websdale (1995) cites several studies that indicate that in rural areas women's roles tend to be more traditional and focused on home and children, and those roles are reinforced by family and friends, men and women. The power imbalance and emphasis on the wife's disobedience associated with traditional roles are related to a higher risk of battering. In rural areas, fundamentalist religious beliefs tend to be more influential and widespread and add to support for women's duties as traditional wives and mothers. In addition, families tend to be more isolated from one another geographically, there is often easy access to weapons, and the limited confidentiality in small towns can be a barrier to seeking help. All these conditions have been associated with increased risk of physical abuse.

Physical and Mental Health

A battered woman's physical health issues may be both batterer-generated and life-generated risks. Along with possible physical injuries caused by her partner's violence, a battered woman may face other physical health issues such as cancer, lupus, asthma, diabetes, or heart disease. These health issues, along with disabilities such as hearing or visual impairment or impaired intellectual capacity or mobility (e.g., needing a wheelchair), make the options available to a battered woman more limited. They can affect her ability to communicate her needs and to access services. Disabilities can also add pressure to comply with an abusive partner's demands when women believe their disability will prevent them from finding another partner (e.g., Chenoweth, 1996).

In addition, battered women's physical health issues may be exacerbated by their abusive partners' behavior. Batterers may prevent women from going to the doctor, fully informing the doctor about her condition, or following a prescribed treatment plan, such as prescription medication or physical therapy. Or a batterer may make his partner's current injury worse. For example, he might wrench the arthritic joints in his partner's arm.

A battered woman's risk analysis of physical health issues might include how she will get help for her health problem, how she will pay for that help, and whether it temporarily or permanently disables her in some way. If a woman faces such a disability, she will consider how it may affect her options and plans. How will it affect her abilities? Will she need a caretaker? For how long? Will she be able to survive without her partner's help? Will she be able to protect herself from her partner's physical attacks? Will it keep her from working for a period of time or permanently? Will she face discrimination and bias? A battered woman will also consider how her partner may use her physical health to further his control. For example, she may rely on him as a caretaker. In addition, he may make it more difficult for her to obtain the resources she needs to lessen her health-related dependence on others.

Unlike physical health, battered women's mental health is controversial. Not too long ago, researchers explored the question of whether women's mental health difficulties contributed to their abuse, or the abuse caused the mental health problems (Kleckner, 1978; Shainess, 1977). The controversy comes with labels for these effects, because such labels have ramifications: the inappropriate stigma of mental disability, negative assumptions about a woman's parenting, questions about her decision-making ability, and ineligibility for certain social services. Evidence about women's psychological *reactions* to abuse is described briefly in Chapter 3, "Batterer-Generated Risks." Battered women who experienced mental health issues or intellectual challenges *before* they were abused by their partner may find that they have more limited options available to them. For example, access to jobs or services may be more complicated for women with a long history of mental health treatment. Concerns about losing custody of their children may be heightened. They may also be more vulnerable to frequent physical assaults. Furthermore, abusers may use mental health issues against their partners: "Who would believe a woman labeled a schizophrenic?"

Unfortunately, some of the labels do accurately describe some aspects of battered women's lives. Whether life generated or batterer generated or both, the risks some battered women experience include mental health issues such as drug and alcohol addiction, depression, anxiety, and posttraumatic stress disorder.

Battered women's health issues may affect their risk analysis and decision making. Advocates should not make assumptions about women's abilities. Some women with health issues are fully able, whereas others may face additional challenges. For example, women who have been overprotected by families or institutions may be unprepared for handling difficult, real-world situations (Chenoweth, 1996). Understanding how health issues affect analysis and planning is an important aspect of woman-defined advocacy and is discussed in further detail in Chapter 6, "Risk Analysis."

Inadequate Responses by Major Social Institutions

Historically, battered women have not been well served by the major social institutions to which they might be expected to turn for help (Dobash & Dobash, 1992). In particular, the police and courts, hospitals and other medical settings, religious institutions, and social service and counseling agencies have been noted for their general neglect of battered women and their needs until recently (Gordon, 1996). Although public education and policy changes have made these systems more responsive in many locations, much of the change is still in process and as yet untested.

Research conducted since the 1960s has shown consistently that most police departments have policies supporting selective responses to calls about battering, with arrest only in the cases of the most severe injuries (e.g., Berk & Loseke, 1980-81; Loving, 1980). Ferraro (1989), for example, conducted a study in which she rode with police as they responded to calls. She reports:

> Most officers expressed frustration with "family fight" calls, and believed there was little that law enforcement could do to stop wife beating. None of the officers liked to go to family fights, because they were perceived as no-win situations. The mandate of the police, according to officers, is to maintain public order and peace. This mandate is consistent with responding to family fight calls only insofar as the "fight" impinges on public peace and order. (p. 167)

More recently, Rigakos (1995) studied police response in another site. He writes:

> Delta police officers hold perceptions of battered women that are sometimes denigrating and often negative. Adopting societal definitions of women as manipulators and liars, the police hold skeptical views of women who protest against their treatment by intimates. (p. 237)

Other researchers have found that, instead of being based on negative views of women, the selective response of police officers, especially experienced ones, stems from their concerns about efficiency and the effective use of resources. That is, if police think that a woman will not cooperate with prosecution or will not make a credible witness, they are less likely to make an arrest (Stalans & Finn, 1995). Even this research has found that visible injury is a prime criterion of credibility, and that police rely on a stereotypical image of mental illness in deciding about arrest. When a woman appears "unstable," police are less likely to arrest her partner. Furthermore, women's alcohol use also undermines their credibility with officers, but does not affect officers' judgments of men (Stalans & Finn, 1995). Whatever the reason for their selectivity, police officers have often not contributed to the protection battered women have sought. Until the past 10 years, with the increasing passage of mandatory arrest laws, statutes in many locations even prevented police from making arrests in misdemeanor cases unless they personally witnessed the violence (Lerman, 1986).

Criminal and civil courts have often been no more responsive, even when an arrest has been made (Ferraro, 1993). Conviction rates vary dramatically, as prosecutors and other personnel, using patterns similar to those found among police, make decisions about pursuing the legal remedies available. Rauma (1984) found that prosecutors were often reluctant to pursue cases because success was most likely when victims were identifiably "good" and defendants were clearly "bad." Dutton (1988) reviewed conviction rates in four sites and found that 53% of the wife abuse defendants were convicted. In sites with large proportions of misdemeanor arrests, conviction rates may be 12% or lower (Lyon & Mace, 1991). In addition, some researchers have documented court reluctance to enforce orders that remove batterers from the home, particularly when they are the legal owners (Finn & Colson, 1990). Even the most recent research on mandatory arrest and protective orders has not shown that these legal system responses work consistently to increase women's safety (e.g., Adhikari, Reinhard, & Johnson, 1993; Buzawa & Buzawa, 1996). Finally, courts have not always been sympathetic to battered women or their children in decisions about custody and visitation of children during divorce proceedings (Walker & Edwall, 1987). The history of legal protection for battered women, then, has often been characterized by inconsistency and avoidance, except in the most extreme cases.

Similarly, the response to battered women in hospitals and other medical settings has historically focused on the narrow treatment of injuries without adequately exploring their cause or providing other interventions that could offer support and possible prevention of further abuse (McLeer & Anwar, 1989). Stark, Flitcraft, and Frazier's (1979) pioneering study of women's treatment in emergency departments found that battered women returned again and again for treatment until the staff began to consider the women to be the problem and to find their stories lacking in credibility. Kurz (1987) and Warshaw (1993) report similar findings. Despite growing attention to woman abuse by the medical community in recent years, studies continue to find that it is often not documented as a cause of injury (Abbott, Johnson, Koziol-McLain, & Lowenstein, 1995).

Although religious faith can be an important source of support for some battered women, many religious institutions have not developed policies and training to respond fully to battered women's needs. For example, a survey of 281 religious leaders in Arizona found that only a third had an explicit policy regarding family violence and less than a third had received specific training about child abuse or battering (J. Johnson, 1992). A follow-up study found that even fewer had a policy, but that more had received some specialized training (Johnson & Bondurant, 1992).

Finally, social service and counseling agencies, to which many women have turned for help with their emotional reactions to abuse, have also commonly failed to respond effectively. Many therapists, for example, have focused on battering from a family systems perspective, which attempts to address the problematic interaction between the couple and can consider the violence a symptom of a larger problem and therefore less important (Bograd, 1984), or assign responsibility for the abuse to the couple rather than to the batterer (Cook & Frantz-Cook, 1984). Therapy that focuses on the reasons a woman has "chosen" an abusive partner, or labels her *codependent* or *addicted* to the violent relationship, has been common until recently and often counterproductive (Dutton, 1992; Koss et al., 1994). Recent research on therapists has raised questions about the understanding some have of the seriousness of battering and the effectiveness of intervention. For example, Hansen, Harway, and Cervantes (1991) provided 362 family therapists with actual cases and asked them to describe them. Forty percent of the therapists did not mention the violence, and of those who did, more than 90% minimized it. Over half said they would not intervene in the violence, and only 11% indicated they would take any steps to help protect the woman. Although many service providers and therapists have been sensitive and committed to their work with battered women, others have contributed to approaches to battering that lead women to feel responsible or have ignored women's danger.

Lorrie

Lorrie has been in psychotherapy and taking medication for psychological problems for years. Lorrie's partner, Phil, beats and rapes Lorrie. Lorrie has called the police in the past. The first time she called, Phil told her she better tell them nothing happened because they'd never believe a crazy woman anyway and they'd probably end up taking her off to the hospital. When they arrived, she told them she and Phil had just had an argument and nothing really happened. The next time she called, she told the police everything. They believed her until Phil explained to them that Lorrie was crazy, showed them her prescription bottles, and told them she just needed to take her medicine. Lorrie left Phil and moved into her own apartment. He broke into her apartment, beat her, and raped her. Visibly bruised, she went to the police and told them to call her therapist if they didn't believe her. Phil was arrested. Lorrie cooperated fully with the prosecutor because she wanted Phil to do some jail time for what he'd done to her. The prosecutor decided to plea bargain the case to a lesser charge with a sentence of 6 months probation only. The prosecutor told Lorrie he decided to bargain because her "mental history" made her a bad witness.

The prosecutor's perception that people with "mental histories" are bad witnesses is the result of misunderstanding and prejudice against persons with mental health issues. If a witness's credibility were the concern, then an exploration of the mental health issues and how they might or might not affect credibility should be part of the investigation and preparation of the case—just as it would with any witness.

Whether Lorrie's mental health issues are batterer generated, life generated, or both, they were used by Phil to further his control. Phil used the threat that no one would believe her to keep Lorrie from telling the police what happened. The next time, Phil used Lorrie's mental health issues to convince the police that he should not be arrested. Finally, Phil benefited from misconceptions regarding people with mental health issues as witnesses and received a lesser charge and sentence. Both Lorrie and Phil now know how the criminal legal system will respond to Lorrie's request for help. This may give Phil additional motivation to terrorize her in the future.

Discrimination Based on Race, Ethnicity, Gender, Sexual Orientation, or Other Bias

Another source of life-generated risks stems from patterns of discrimination in U.S. society. Discrimination can be understood as treatment that denies access to services or resources, involves harsh judgments, or invokes more difficult standards of credibility or performance. It is a pattern of biased behavior directed at people because of their membership in or association with a larger group that has particular characteristics. Such characteristics can be temporary, as when people are discriminated against because they are too young, or permanent, as in discrimination based on race or ethnicity or gender;

they can be totally beyond the individual's control, as in discrimination against people who are very tall, or partly changeable with effort, as in learning disabilities. Among the most common targets of discrimination in American society are people who do not have European or Anglo ancestry, such as African Americans, Latinos or Hispanics, Asian Americans (including people of Japanese, Chinese, and Vietnamese ancestry), and Native Americans; women; and people who identify themselves as lesbian or gay. Of course, many other groups experience discrimination, such as the elderly and people who have some form of physical or mental "disability." Many of the types of complications described for battered women who also experience one of the forms of discrimination addressed in this section would apply to other forms of discrimination as well.

Discrimination takes different forms for different groups and affects members of those groups in various ways. For example, people whose group membership is visible or known are more likely to be affected by job and income limitations. African Americans who had full-time jobs in 1996 earned less than 77% of Anglos' income, whereas Hispanics received 67% of Anglos' income (*Employment and Earnings*, 1997). Furthermore, unemployment rates for African American adults age 25 and older were nearly twice the rate of Anglos, and increased substantially when 16- to 24-year-olds were included (*Employment and Earnings*, 1997). People whose group membership is not visible, such as lesbians and gays who are not "out," are much less likely to experience this form of overt discrimination, but have to deal with many other work-related concerns as part of remaining "closeted." This is also true for undocumented immigrants, people who are afraid to disclose a health condition, and others.

Of course, discrimination affects many other areas of life, such as access to housing, education and training, and other resources and services. Every institution—health care, legal system, family, education, public and private social services, and others—is implicated. Therefore, the experience of discrimination is unavoidable for the groups affected. In addition, all forms of possible and experienced discrimination taken together often have an effect on group members' self-confidence and sense of self-worth.

What all this means for battered women is that discrimination that affects them as women is even more complex when they are also members of other groups that experience discrimination. Women of color, for example, have higher rates of unemployment and lower incomes, on average, than Anglo women. They may have many fewer alternatives and much more complex considerations in their risk analyses as a result of all the types of "double discrimination" they may encounter. Crenshaw (1994) calls the shared effect of race and ethnicity and gender "intersectionality," and the term can be applied to women who experience discrimination for other reasons as well.

Among the effects of intersectionality may be a reluctance on the part of battered women to tell anyone about their abuse because they do not want to raise questions or contribute to further discrimination against other members of the group (Dasgupta & Warrier, 1996). As Kanuha (1996) writes:

> The basic nature of prejudice and oppression requires that marginalized individuals and groups lessen the conditions for their oppression by minimizing any part of their identity, behavior, history, values . . . that may be construed as deviant. (p. 43)

Talking specifically about the effect on battered women of color, she continues:

> The activity of protecting men of color who are batterers from further racial stigmatization has in fact resulted in our collusion with their gendered violence. Somehow, both the antiviolence movement and communities of color have claimed through default that it is more important for men of color to be protected in all aspects of their lives than it is for women of color to be protected in the most intimate and private aspects of their lives. (p. 44)

Battered women who are immigrants face particularly complex life-generated risks: "The typical problems of a battering relationship are further complicated by issues of gender, race, socioeconomic status, immigration status, and language" (Orloff et al., 1995, p. 314). If their partners are also immigrants, the women may be reluctant to seek protection and potentially jeopardize the tenuous status they both hold. More commonly, however, battered immigrant women have partners who are citizens, and fear the legal system and possible detention or deportation should they file a complaint. In addition, achieving financial independence is much more difficult.

In general, battered women who are further marginalized by other identities may find resources limited for multiple reasons. Among the reasons is that the necessary services are often lacking. Citing several studies, Koss et al. (1994) observe, "Community support systems do a poor job of serving certain groups of battered women, including minorities, immigrants (both documented and undocumented), lesbians, and women with mental and physical disabilities" (p. 96).

Donna

Donna and Mark have been married for 10 years. Mark is a school teacher. Donna also worked full time as a teacher, but now works part time in the school system, giving music lessons, so she can be home for their two children. Donna and Mark are African American. Mark is "in charge" at home, making all major family decisions, controlling the money, and telling Donna when and where she can go. He is very jealous and often accuses Donna of having affairs. Several times a year, Mark hits Donna to "let her know who's boss." Last time, her son tried to stop Mark and Mark shoved him out of the way. Donna, concerned for her children, told Mark she thinks he needs some help and that she'd be willing to go to marital counseling with him. Mark told her, "therapy is for white people" and then repeated the same phrases he says to Donna every time he hits her. "Don't tell anyone about our business. You know they'd just love to have an excuse to fire a black man from a good job, throw him in jail, and split up another black family. Just keep your mouth shut."

Donna's risk analysis. Donna's risk analysis is intertwined with her assessment of how racism will affect her options and add to her risks:

- Donna believes Mark is right. If what he is doing to her gets out, he would probably lose his job and would not be able to find another one.
- The child protection people might get involved and Donna does not know what they would do in her situation. They might try to make Mark move out of the house or, even worse, force her to move out or try to take the kids away. As a teacher, she has dealt with them and knows they are tough on black mothers.
- Donna understands that Mark uses the realities of racism to further his control by keeping her from talking to anyone about her marriage, her children, and Mark's behavior.

Batterers' Manipulation of Life-Generated Risks

Not only are battered women made more vulnerable by the host of life-generated risks, but their abusive partners are often aware of these risks and manipulate them to reinforce their power and control. For example, in her study of African American battered women, Richie (1996) notes that "the African American men used the fact of their overrepresentation in the criminal justice system and other racial rhetoric to strike a chord of sympathy with the African American battered women" (p. 121), thereby discouraging calls to police.

Batterers of immigrant women may also invoke the legal system to maintain their control, as Orloff et al. (1995) observe:

> In domestic violence cases, batterers manipulate these beliefs to coerce their partners into dropping charges or dismissing protection order petitions. The abusers may convince the battered woman that because the batterer is a citizen, has more money, and is a man, he is therefore more credible and will win in court. (p. 316)

Batterers may use threats to amplify women's concerns about the legal system and the possible loss of custody of their children to try to keep women from leaving. Divorce is a primary context in which such threats occur, as Kurz (1995) and other researchers (e.g., Arendell, 1995) report. Kurz found that a quarter of the women in her sample of divorced mothers who had been afraid of their husbands were still worried that their ex-husbands could take their children. Arendell (1995) found that the fathers in her study filed for custody explicitly to harass their former wives.

Custody issues can be used even more manipulatively when the battered woman and her partner are not married and there are other sources of concern about publicity, as can occur in lesbian battering. As Renzetti (1992) found, for lesbians, leaving a battering relationship may mean having to leave without the children—especially if the batterer is the biological parent. In most cases, the relationship is not legally recognized, and therefore only one parent can have legal custody:

> However, even battered lesbians who are the biological parents of their children confront the fear of losing those children. Batterers may threaten to expose their partners' lesbian identity, which carries the additional threat that their children may be taken out of the home by the state because they are lesbians. . . . Children may be used by batterers as a means to manipulate their partners into staying, or concerns about the children's well being may prevent the abused partners from leaving. (p. 84)

Battered women's risk analyses, then, occur in the context of real life-generated risks and their partners' manipulative threats, which reinforce the risks and increase the complexity of seeking help. When battered women are also members of other "marginalized" or stigmatized groups, the path to safety becomes even more treacherous.

Women's Perception of Public Resource Response

Battered women's perceptions of how public resources treat a larger group of which they may be members is another significant factor in risk analyses and plans. These larger groups might include women, battered women, women of color, immigrant women, women with disabilities, lesbians, women who do not speak English, low-income women, women who live in a certain area or neighborhoods, and others. Battered women's perceptions may be based on past experience with a particular resource, what they have heard from others who have used the services, or their own assumptions and judgments. As Renzetti (1992) observes, "Many sources of help available to heterosexual victims are not perceived by lesbians to be sources of help available to them" (p. 88).

For example, a battered woman who speaks only Spanish may assume that a service that has no Spanish-speaking staff will be unresponsive to her, or an Asian battered woman may assume that an agency located outside the predominantly Asian community in her city will be less understanding of her culture. As Richie (1996; see also Dasgupta & Warrier, 1996; Huisman, 1996) found in her study,

> the African American battered women were less likely than the white women to use social services, battered women's programs, or to go to the hospital. . . . Other reasons that the African American battered women reported not reaching out for help included a general mistrust of social services based on previous experiences, the batterers' control of their mobility and phone use, and their own involvement in criminal activities. (p. 94)

Each battered woman may identify with several groups, and her perception of service providers' potential insensitivity, ignorance, or bias toward any of the groups will affect her plans.

All battered women belong to at least two groups—women and battered women. If public resources are perceived to be insensitive or ignorant about women or the nature and realities of domestic violence, then battered women may avoid including such resources in their plans. For example, it may be well-known in the community that a prosecutor seeks dismissals in all but a few "serious" cases because he believes 95% of domestic violence is as much the battered woman's fault as the batterer's—after all, says this prosecutor, "she stays in the relationship and it takes two to tango." Battered women who are aware of the prosecutor's view would probably not choose to include prosecution in their safety planning strategies.

Battered women of color may consider how their race will affect the response they or their partners will experience. Will law enforcement and the legal system believe them, take the violence seriously, respond quickly to their call, arrest them too, treat their partners fairly? Will social service agencies be sensitive to their family, will their children be inappropriately taken from them? Will they be given a fair chance to get employment, training, education?

Carol

Carol, an African American battered woman, is thinking about leaving her husband and filing for divorce. She is concerned that he may react violently when he receives the papers, so she's thinking about hiding from him for a few weeks. Carol talks to a friend of hers who she knows went to a local domestic violence shelter to get away from her violent partner. Her friend tells Carol it was a good place to hide if you need to, but she doesn't think she'd go there again. Her friend reports that staff at the shelter are all white, except for one Latina, and they don't seem to listen to her. The staff doesn't leave you alone, they keep trying to get you to do things they want you to do, and they don't understand the issues African American women have to deal with. They were very judgmental about how African American women in the shelter treat their children and, her friend says, the staff even reported one of the women to child protective services. For Carol, the local domestic violence shelter will probably not be part of her safety plans because she may be worried that at best she will be misunderstood and at worst her family will be reported to child protective services.

Battered women with disabilities may consider how their disability might affect the response. Will the service providers assume I have less ability than I do, or assume I have more? Will services be physically accessible? Will they understand how a disability may affect safety planning and decision making? Is the staff knowledgeable about mental disabilities? Will they work with me or will I be labeled and rejected? Will my disability be used against me? Will my partner or the state be able to take my children from me because I asked for help? Will I be blamed for my addiction? Will I have to give up my children to get help from certain services? If I have the choice, should I hide my disability or disclose it?

A battered lesbian may consider how her sexual orientation will affect the response. If she believes the response may be negative, she may consider whether she will be able to "hide" the true nature of her relationship with her abusive partner. Will I be welcome at social service agencies? Will they still try to help me once they know my partner is a woman? Will their ignorance or hatred of lesbians keep them from giving me the help I need? Will law enforcement take my complaint seriously? Will the laws and courts respond to me? Will I be ridiculed, harassed, threatened? Will "coming out" to get help make other things in my life worse? Will I lose my job, my housing, my friends?

Liz

Liz is trying to figure out what to do the next time her ex-partner hits her. Last time Liz's ex-partner came over to her apartment and started beating her, she almost called the police because she was afraid she would be seriously injured. Her ex-partner yelled at her, "Go ahead—call the police—what do you think they're going to do when I tell them we're gay?" To find out, Liz calls an attorney. The attorney's advice is to keep the police and courts out of it, saying, "You just won't know what the reaction might be. It'll depend on the person; some police and court personnel might be sensitive and helpful and others may refuse to help and treat you very badly." Liz's perception of the police and court response, developed on the advice of an attorney, is that using them will be a risky plan, and she may therefore eliminate the strategy of calling the police unless the violence is so great and she simply has no other choice.

Implications for Advocacy

Elements of Woman-Defined Advocacy

1. Understand a battered woman's perspective, including her risk analysis and safety plan.
   - Understand how life-generated risks affect a battered woman's risk analysis and plans.
     - ⅃ Identify how her abusive partner may manipulate such risks to further his control.

Identify life-generated risks and understand how a battered woman is including them in her risk analysis. Consider asking such questions as,

- Besides the trouble with your partner, what are you worried about now?
- What do you think would happen if you tried to [fill in the blank]?

Understand how a batterer is using life-generated risks to further his control. This issue is most likely to come to light when an advocate is discussing a particular option with a woman. The woman could be reluctant to pursue an option because of her partner's manipulation of a life-generated risk (see Figure 4.1).

Be aware of the reality of bias and discrimination. Learning about the reality of bias and discrimination is the advocate's responsibility. Advocates may learn from individual battered women and from others about the realities that certain groups of battered women face. Do not presume a barrier, however. It may not be an issue.

Be aware of women's perceptions of how discrimination based on race, ethnicity, gender, disability, or sexual orientation may be a risk for them. Discovering women's perceptions is the advocate's responsibility.

Note

1. In 1996, women constituted 46.2% of the paid labor force, and the percentage has been growing consistently (*Employment and Earnings*, 1997, p. 171). According to current projections, women's involvement in paid work will grow at twice the rate of men's between 1994 and 2005 (Fullerton, 1995).

Possible Effects of Life-Generated Risks	Possible Uses of Life-Generated Risks by Batterer
Financial limitations	
• Mobility • Job choice • Transportation • Availability of telephone—adds to isolation and fewer safety options • Health care • Housing options • Getting credit	• Use financial constraints to limit her independence and further her isolation, e.g., can't go out, make phone calls, have a car • Could use to reinforce the message that she couldn't afford to live without him
Home location: where women live	
• Resources may be unavailable • Lack of transportation may limit options	• Use resource limitation to further control
Physical health issues	
• Services or resources may be inaccessible • People may inaccurately judge a woman's ability • Women may face discrimination and bias	• Could use the disability to keep her trapped and isolated • Could remove devices that increase her mobility • Use her disability as topic to humiliate and abuse • Threaten or remove access to caretaker, if relevant
Mental health issues	
• Services or resources may be inaccessible • People may inaccurately judge a woman's ability • Women may face discrimination and bias	• Use her disability as topic to humiliate and abuse • Threaten or use her disability to have her hospitalized, medicated, labeled • Threaten or use her disability to keep her from getting custody or access to her children
Inadequate responses by major social institutions	
• May keep women from seeking help • May lead to ineffective response • May lead to insensitive responses • May keep women from getting any help from the institution	• Failure to help her may reinforce his control • If she doesn't believe system will help, she has fewer options for safety *(continued)*

Figure 4.1. Battered Women's Analysis of Life-Generated Risks

Possible Effects of Life-Generated Risks	Possible Uses of Life-Generated Risks by Batterer
Discrimination based on race, ethnicity, gender, sexual preference or other bias	
• Keep people from believing what women are telling them that can lead to ineffective or harmful responses from legal system and others responding to battered women • Keep women from getting or advancing in employment • Keep women from living where they want to live • Keep women from disclosing the violence • Keep women from getting credit, loans, mortgages • Keep women from accessing the help they need • Lead women to believe no one will help them and they may not receive help • Keep women from defending themselves for fear they are more likely to be arrested, convicted, and incarcerated or lose their children • Keep women from getting effective health care, substance abuse treatment • Keep women from educational opportunities	• Use the woman's perception of discrimination to convince her she has few options and resources • Benefits from the reality of discrimination that limits his partner's options or resources • Use the possibility that he will be discriminated against to convince his partner not to seek help, particularly from law enforcement • Lesbian or gay partner uses the threat of disclosure of the relationship and potential resulting harm to control partner • Benefits from the negative messages of bias and discrimination that can reinforce his devaluing of her

Figure 4.1.   Continued

5

Battered Women's Decision Making and Safety Plans

W hen battered women analyze risks, they also think about how to reduce them. Safety planning is sometimes seen as an advocate-initiated process, but this view ignores battered women's active and ongoing safety planning processes. Although these topics are addressed separately here, women's risk analysis and safety planning are intertwined. This chapter describes the context of battered women's decision making and identifies the key components of women's safety plans and the types of strategies women include in them.

Battered Women's Decision Making

Research on battered women's decision making has emphasized decisions about whether or not to leave the relationship with the abusive partner. Much understanding of battered women's behavior and analyses has focused on women who do not leave a battering relationship immediately and their apparent passivity in the face of physical danger. Some researchers and other observers who have adopted this view regard battered women's behavior as a sign of *learned helplessness* (Seligman, 1975). Others have focused instead on the continuing, active efforts battered women make to understand their situation and to provide for the safety of themselves and their children—what some have called the *survivor theory* (Dutton, 1996a; Gondolf & Fisher, 1988; Hoff, 1990). The approach of this book is consistent with a view of battered women as active decision makers who seek the help that appears available and appropriate to their circumstances.

It should be clear by now that as women weigh their options, their alternatives and the decisions they face are more complex than simply staying or leaving. Furthermore, it should be clear that remaining in the relationship does not necessarily mean acceptance of the violence, and that leaving the relationship does not necessarily mean that the violence will end or other risks will be reduced, despite the social expectations to that effect. Mahoney (1994) summarizes these points effectively:

> When women experience violence in intimate relationships, we [battered women] assert ourselves in a variety of ways. We attempt to change the situation and improve the relationship; we seek help formally or informally from friends, family, or organizations; we flee temporarily and make return conditional upon assurances of care and safety; we break off relationships. Continuing the relationship may therefore be part of a pattern of resistance to violence on the part of the woman.
>
> On the other hand, a woman may continue the relationship because of uncertainty about other options or her ability to subsist or care for dependents, because of depression and dislocation that come with intimate loss and harm, or because she is afraid that leaving will trigger lethal danger—because, essentially, she is held captive. (p. 73)

Studies over the past two decades have consistently shown that women typically try many strategies to deal with their partner's violence, and that they can be very resourceful (Brown, 1997; Dobash & Dobash, 1979; Koss et al., 1994). Over time, their experience with these strategies and their partner's behavior affect their analysis of their alternatives and the new decisions they make. Early studies found that many battered women react to their first experience of violence with shock, and then attempt to make sense of the event (Bograd, 1988). The way they come to understand the event then affects what they do.

For example, Frieze (1979) found that battered women varied in their perceptions about violence. Some thought it was attributable to their partners, whereas others thought it was their own fault. Women also varied in their analysis of abuse "stability": Some thought it was likely to change, whereas others thought it was not. The women who regarded the violence as due to their partners and as unlikely to change were more likely to say they wanted to leave the relationship than those who saw it as a temporary, unusual occurrence or their own fault.

Similarly, Ferraro and Johnson (1983) studied 120 women in a shelter and found that six types of rationalization were common at the initial stage. They note that these rationalizations were often rejected over time in response to changed circumstances. The most important of these changes were increased violence, changes in available resources, changes in commitment to the relationship, loss of hope that things would improve, increased visibility of the violence, and others' responses. Over time, many women shifted their analysis from seeing the violence as something temporary, something they could change by modifying their behavior, to seeing it as a more stable behavior pattern of their partner. With this change in analysis, they were more likely to increase help seeking and to consider more dramatic options, including leaving.

Some studies have found that women initially rely on their own resources and are most likely to turn to others for help only when their sense of personal danger has escalated (e.g., Lempert, 1996; Mills, 1985). Lempert (1996), for example, found that the women she interviewed first tried to contain the violence and keep it invisible before moving to other strategies. In these ways, the women tried to keep themselves physically safe and avoid being seen as a "victim." Bowker (1983) conducted one of the earliest studies of help seeking through interviews with 146 formerly battered women. He found that women reported substantial efforts after the most recent incident they experienced. Fifty-two percent contacted friends, 49% tried lawyers, 43% called family, 43% tried social service agencies, 36% contacted women's groups, 34% called the police, and 29% contacted shelters. Overall, these women reported that the shelters were the most helpful resource they had found.

Gondolf and Fisher (1988) completed one of the largest studies of women's help seeking. They studied more than 6,000 women who entered shelters in Texas in 1984 and 1985. They found that the women averaged nearly five different types of help seeking prior to entering the shelter, and almost three formal or informal types of contacts. Seventy-one percent had previously left home, 53% had called the police at least once, 47% had called family members, and 47% had called friends. Gondolf and Fisher also found that women's efforts to obtain help intensified when the violence became more frequent or severe—a finding that is not consistent with the learned helplessness model of battered women's behavior.

In general, the research provides extensive evidence of the complexity of battered women's evaluations of their relationships and their subsequent decision making. For many women, commitment to the relationship is an early prime influence (cf. Barnett & LaViolette, 1993), and their hope that the violence will not be repeated or that their partner will change dominates. Several studies (e.g., Marden & Rice, 1995) document women's use of hope as a major coping strategy. Sometimes women remain hopeful because they are committed to their partner and sometimes because the alternatives they see are inadequate. In any case, hope for their partners' change remains a powerful part of early decision making for many battered women.

Pagelow (1981) found that 73% of a shelter sample returned to their partner because he had apologized and they hoped he would change. Barnett and Lopez-Real (1985, cited in Barnett & LaViolette, 1993) found that "hoped partner would change" was the primary reason battered women said they stayed with their partners. Related research (e.g., Okun, 1986) found that partners' involvement in counseling was a major factor in women returning to their partners after time in a shelter. Gondolf and Fisher (1988), in fact, found that "batterer in counseling" was the single strongest influence in women's decisions to return to their partners, even when other factors were controlled statistically.

Other research and clinical experience describe a balancing of hope and fear as primary to the decision-making process. Ginny NiCarthy (1987) uses the following language:

> During the course of the relationship the women had made decisions by balancing their fear of staying against the hope for an improved relationship without the partner, or weighing the hope for change in the relationship with their fear of living alone. Although they didn't necessarily state it that way, many left when there was a shift in the balance of fear or hope. (p. 315)

Other researchers have found different turning points in the decision-making process. Kirkwood (1993; see also Lempert, 1995), for example, discusses the importance of the woman's awareness that the abuse has had a negative effect on her ways of acting and thinking about herself.

Women's experience with resources is another important factor in their decision making. As already indicated, women commonly turn to family and friends. Their reactions help the women define their situation, weigh alternatives, and determine strategies. What the battered woman tells and asks those friends, how she describes what is happening, and what help she is looking for may vary greatly. Some battered women may describe the violence, the threats, and the risks in great and accurate detail, whereas others may speak more euphemistically, talking about marital problems, their partner's temper, or that they are under a lot of stress. This language may be a way to "test" the person they are talking to, to see if she or he will be sympathetic and understanding or somehow shocked and distancing.

In addition, a battered woman may have a deep spiritual or religious belief and faith that provides both strength and direction. A battered woman's faith may give her the courage to face her risks, make decisions, and implement her plans to protect herself and her children. In addition to providing support, a religious belief may favor certain decisions and preclude others. For example, a religious belief might be that a battered woman must stay in the relationship, hold the family together, and try to "make it work." Other religious beliefs could lead to different directives.

Formal helping sources, such as shelters, are significant helping sources to women who use them. Women who use shelters tend to be poorer and have less education and job experience than battered women who do not (Gondolf & Fisher, 1988). Shelters provide time, safety, information, and help with community resources, as well as the experience of functioning away from the partner. They also have been found, when combined with other help-seeking activities, to help shift the balance of power within the relationship, at least temporarily (Bowker et al., 1988). Similarly, Kemp et al. (1995) found that perceived social support was related to lower levels of psychological symptoms. Sullivan (1991) found that advocate support to women who left a shelter to return to their partners encouraged women's more active use of community resources. Follow-up research also found that advocate support to women contributed to reduced depression over time (Campbell, Sullivan, & Davidson, 1995). Supportive services, then, may often be complementary and cumulative in their effect.

Fischer and Rose (1995) found that one of the reasons the women in their study filed for a protective order was that the abuse was becoming more serious and was affecting the children. Fisher and Rose indicate that seeking a protective order was a last resort, to which the women turned only after other efforts to stop the abuse had failed. In this study, the women indicated that among the other motivations for seeking a protective order were a desire for external validation, a mechanism to communicate loudly and clearly that they were serious, and a public record of the abuse and their effort to stop it. All these goals contributed to enhancing their power in the relationship. Many of the women then "dropped" the order, feeling that they had obtained more control and they wanted to give their partner another chance.

Increasingly, investigators have concluded that it is critical to understand the combination of larger social and personal and individual features of the woman's situation to comprehend her reaction (Carlisle-Frank, 1991). For example, as we showed in Chapter 4, "Life-Generated Risks," differences in decision making attributable partly to a woman's race or ethnicity may be critical. Bachman and Coker (1995) studied 1,535 female "victims of intimate-perpetrated violence" and found that, other factors being equal, African American women were more likely than others to make reports to the police. As with seeking shelter and obtaining protective orders, arrest can be a strategy used as part of a woman's effort to communicate her seriousness and increase her power in the relationship (Fischer & Rose, 1995).

Clearly, battered women's analyses and decisions are complex and change over time. They vary with the individual characteristics of the women, their partners, and their perceptions of the relationship; the individual, social, and organizational resources available; the reactions of significant people and organizations; and the frequency, type, severity, and meaning of the abuse they experience. For example, Herbert, Silver, and Ellard's (1991) study of 130 battered women reports that "responses of women currently involved in abusive relationships suggest that they are viewing their situations in a more positive light than might an outsider" (p. 322). These researchers found that women who saw positive aspects to the relationship, little or no change in the frequency or severity of abuse, and ongoing expressions of love and affection were most likely to remain involved with their abusive partners. Follingstad et al. (1990) found that over half of the 234 women they studied could use their experience of emotional abuse to predict likely physical abuse, and that emotional abuse had a more severe effect on them. Furthermore, Follingstad et al. found that property damage was one of the most powerful predictors of motivation to leave the relationship.

Studies that look at many factors to try to predict leaving have had varied findings. Strube and Barbour (1983), for example, found that women's (declining) commitment to the relationship and their economic independence were the strongest factors associated with leaving. Research has consistently found that economic and other resource considerations are central to the ways battered women think about their options (e.g., Gelles & Straus, 1988; Pagelow, 1981). In one of the larger studies, Gondolf and his associates (Gondolf & Fisher, 1988) analyzed the exit plans of 800 women who had used Texas shelters. After considering many possible factors that could influence women's decisions, they found that three of the four most influential ones related to financial resources: having access to independent transportation, child care, and an independent income. Only 16% of the women with their own income planned to return to their batterers. More recently, economic resources have assumed a significant part in models designed to understand the complexities of battered women's behavior (e.g., Dutton, 1996a). Horton and Johnson (1993) found that women who left had fewer children, more severe and frequent abuse, a more substantial support system, his alcohol use as a contributing factor, and a longer history of abuse than those who stayed in the relationship. Follingstad, Hause, Rutledge, and Polek (1992) observe that women's individual characteristics cannot explain their behavior. Instead, they suggest that women who have left relationships may have experienced different situations than those who remain:

> Women out of the relationship experienced higher frequencies of abuse, had a shorter time lapse between initial involvement in the relationship and the first violent incident and suffered more serious injuries from the first incident than women still in the relationship. These factors probably suggested to the women that the relationship was a dangerous place to be from the outset. . . . Women out of the relationship were less likely to have a batterer who showed remorse or treated the woman better after the abusive event, thus probably helping to make her decision less cluttered with contradictory messages. (p. 126)

In short, no single study has yet been able to include all the potentially influential factors associated with leaving identified by researchers and advocates. Strube (1988) found that research that combines several features of the individuals and their current and past situations is most likely to advance our understanding of the decisions battered women make. Because the combination of abuse (of the woman as well as the children); individual resources; timing; partner's behavior; other features of the relationship; reaction of friends, family, and helping agencies; and the other factors known to play a role for at least some women varies so much, it is probably most helpful simply to know the broad features that support many women in making the best decisions for the safety of themselves and their children.

In general, researchers have found that the process of change for many battered women, including possibly leaving the relationship, can be lengthy.[1] Okun (1986) found that women left their abusive partners an average of five times before leaving permanently. Horton and Johnson (1993) found that it took an average of 8 years for the women who left the relationship to leave permanently, and those who left had suffered worse abuse than those who remained.

Unfortunately, as Mahoney (1994) notes, we know much less about the experiences of battered women who have stayed in relationships with their abusive partners in which the physical violence has stopped. Bowker (1983) is one of the few researchers to study this experience, and he found that it took consistent objections from the women, strong commitment to the relationship from the men, and external resources and support for the women to help shift the balance of power in the relationship.

Overall, the message from these results is that women are active, they plan in many different ways, and their reactions to their partner's violence vary enormously. The message is also that support and information and resources are helpful, even if their effect is not apparent right away or in the form expected (see also Campbell, Miller, Cardwell, & Belknap, 1994). The message is compatible with Ann Jones's (1994) observation that "even a woman who *seems* to be passively complying may be biding her time, waiting for the right moment to escape; she holds her own by *acting* with extreme caution, and she too needs empowering outside help to get free" (p. 181).

Battered Women's Safety Plans

Battered women's decision making and safety planning are complex. Battered women's plans respond to the range of batterer-generated and life-generated risks. Their process of planning may include evaluating whether staying or leaving will reduce or increase risks and how their partners will react. In addition, women will think about their partner's ability and willingness to change. As women plan, they incorporate and reassess information.

To understand the intricacy of women's plans fully, it is helpful to distinguish the common characteristics of most battered women's safety plans, as shown in Figure 5.1: protection strategies, staying strategies, leaving strategies, and short-term and/or long-term time frames. The following discussion of battered women's safety plans uses these characteristics to show their complexity and detail. These different strategies and time frames are intertwined in the plans actually developed by women. A woman's staying strategy may include a protection strategy as well as a long-range time frame for leaving. On the other hand, some battered women's plans may not include all

Protection strategies	Seek to prevent and respond to physical violence.
Staying strategies	Respond to the range of batterer-generated and life-generated risks while a woman remains in her relationship.
Leaving strategies	Respond to the range of batterer-generated and life-generated risks a woman faces as she leaves or after she has left her relationship.
Time frames	May be short-term and/or long-range.

Figure 5.1. Characteristics of Battered Women's Safety Plans

these characteristics. For example, some battered women may plan to escape immediately and therefore would not have a staying strategy. Other women may have no plan to leave.

Protection Strategies

Battered women's protection strategies seek to prevent and respond to physical violence. Three types of immediate protection strategies are fleeing, asking a third party to intervene, and self-defense. Some of these protection strategies are made in advance, and some are developed spontaneously as women are trying to survive a particular attack. Battered women's protection strategies differ depending on the extent of the physical violence, their partners' reaction to the use of the strategy, and the personal and public resources available to the woman.

To flee, a woman may have a prearranged escape path and destination for herself and her children. For example, a battered woman's children may know that when their mother says to them, "Get out of the house," they should run down the street to their grandmother's house or next door to a friend's apartment. Fleeing might also mean keeping a certain door unlocked for a quick exit, climbing out a bathroom window, leaving from work, or leaving once the partner's asleep or has passed out from drinking.

Battered women may also seek to protect themselves by having a third person intervene. This might mean formal intervention by a law enforcement officer or more informal intervention by a relative, neighbor, or friend. This intervention might be prearranged or spontaneous. For example, a battered woman talks to her brother-in-law about her husband's temper. Her brother-in-law tells her to call him the next time his brother gets out of control and he will come over to keep him from hurting her. In other circumstances, a woman calls the police herself or her screams are heard by a passerby who calls the police. A longer-term third-party intervention strategy is to have a friend or family member move in with the family. A battered woman may use this strategy for several reasons: 1) to share costs and reduce the financial stress on the family; 2) because she believes her partner will not hit her in front of this person; or 3) because the person will intervene and protect her and the children.

A battered woman may defend herself by actively trying to minimize the physical injury of the attack or by fighting back. To minimize physical injury, a woman might curl up in a ball, cover her face, or try to block the punches, slaps, or kicks by wearing a thick coat or layers of clothes. She might also try to keep items her partner has used against her in the past out of easy reach, such as baseball bats, knives, or guns. In some situations, a battered woman may act as "the bartender," pouring weak drinks to prevent the partner's drunken anger or strong drinks to get him to pass out before hurting her. A woman may also fight back to defend herself and her children. When women act in self-defense, it is not part of a pattern of coercive control and should not be characterized as battering or "mutual abuse."

Some battered women also develop a variety of protection strategies for their children. A woman might do the following:

- Send the children to a family member, neighbor, or friend to keep them from being abused or from witnessing the abuse. This may be particularly effective if the woman's partner is primarily or only abusive on weekends or other somewhat predictable times.
- Sleep in the children's bedroom to protect herself and her children. This may keep her partner from abusing or sexually abusing the children, or inhibit her partner's attack on her.
- Feed the children early and put them to bed before her partner comes home.
- Never leave the children alone with her partner.
- Involve the children in a lot of activities that take them away from home for periods of time.
- Put the children's room as far away from her and her partner's bedroom as possible because that is the only place he hurts her.

Some battered women may also try to get their partners to change as part of a longer-term protection strategy. To get an abusive partner to change, a woman might do the following:

- Warn her partner she may call the police, tell someone about the abuse, or leave temporarily to let him know she is serious about her demand that he change. Of course, some women may actually take these steps.

- Try to get her partner to get some help by agreeing to go to couples' counseling so he will go. She may also get a friend or family member to try to convince him.
- Turn to the court for help. She may obtain a partial protective order—so her partner is ordered not to hurt her but can remain in the home—or go to court-ordered counseling.

Leaving a relationship may be the most significant protection strategy, particularly if a woman is able to leave and her abusive partner does not know where she has gone or how to find her. This strategy has been the cornerstone of a great deal of domestic violence public response, particularly when shelters and going into hiding were the only responses available. Leaving and going into hiding can be an extremely effective plan to avoid physical violence, particularly as a temporary strategy. As discussed in Chapter 3, "Batterer-Generated Risks," however, leaving may increase other risks in a battered woman's analysis and raise new ones. Children, divorce, and custody or visitation issues may force a woman to identify her whereabouts. The partial or complete loss of contact with family, friends, or community can be an option with harsh personal consequences for the woman and her children.

In addition, leaving does not always reduce or prevent the risk of physical violence. If a woman has left and gone into hiding, her partner may find her. If she's left and her partner knows where she is, he may continue to attack her and may even escalate the violence to try to force her to return. For some women, the "separation violence" is worse than the violence they experience while in the relationship, and for some women it is lethal.

Staying Strategies

Battered women's safety strategies for staying respond to the wide range of batterer-generated and life-generated risks while the woman remains in the relationship; they may be short term or long range. Whether a battered woman plans to leave a relationship tomorrow, in 10 years, or never, she will continue to try to respond to the risks her partner's behavior creates. What women do to stay safe while continuing to deal with an abusive partner is a fairly new focus of advocacy. The exploration of battered women's safety strategies for staying is just beginning. What we do know from several years of informal discussion and use of the woman-defined approach to advocacy is that battered women use incredibly creative, complex, and varied safety plans for themselves and their children. These plans include protection strategies for physical violence, and respond to other batterer-generated and life-generated risks as well.

The following are just some of the safety planning for staying strategies identified to date. While considering these strategies, keep in mind that they may have worked in some way for some women in some circumstances. In addition, they are often developed in the context of having few or no other viable alternatives. Also, a batterer may prevent his partner from implementing a particular strategy; therefore, each battered woman may include different combinations, or none, of these strategies. A battered woman might do the following:

- Get a job or join community or religious groups to have a forum where she is valued, gains self-confidence, and gets support.
- Join a self-defense or physical fitness class.
- Become very involved with her religion to give her the strength and courage to go on.
- Call the domestic violence hotline periodically to check her perspective, explore her options, and get understanding and support.
- Go to a therapist or counselor to help her sort out her problems and figure out what to do.
- Always agree with her partner's point of view, avoid arguments, and try to placate him. Attempts to "keep him happy," "give him what he wants," "try to be the perfect wife or mother" might also be considered safety strategies for staying.
- Carefully preserve her support system. For example, she might "rotate" the friends she turns to for support, "so no one gets sick of me."
- Not get her family or friends involved if she believes her partner may physically hurt them.
- Develop complex ways to have contact with family or friends without her partner knowing.

To address financial risks, a battered woman might do the following:

- Work outside the home to have access to some money of her own.
- Siphon off some of the money he "gives" her for household expenses.
- Have money taken directly from her paycheck to pay the rent or mortgage to keep her partner from spending it on other things.
- Have bank accounts or safety deposit boxes her partner doesn't know about.
- Ask friends to hold money for her.
- Ask family members to have accounts for her children that her partner cannot get access to.

- Have a life insurance policy or other strategy to preserve assets for the children.

There are, of course, consequences for each of these staying strategies. Some coping tactics will have negative effects on the woman and possibly her children. For example, if she drinks to calm her anxiety and numb the pain, she may develop an addiction. Continuous deference to her partner may affect a woman's self-confidence and ability to be independent. Staying to preserve her children's financial security may mean they will continue to witness the physical violence against her, as well as be influenced by their parents' unequal relationship.

Identifying and listing safety strategies for staying is not an endorsement of women living in violent relationships. Certainly, women should not have to hide, "walk on eggshells," constantly plan, and alter their entire lives to reduce or survive batterer-generated risks. This is the reality for many battered women, however—at times because there is no other choice and at times because the strategy "works."

Lorin

Lorin has three children, ages 2, 5, and 7. John, her husband, is the father of her youngest child. The father of her two older children died 2 years ago. She quit her minimum wage job when she married John. She and her children rely exclusively on John's small income and even more on the generosity of her in-laws, who give them money and allow them to live rent free in a house they own. John beats her and cheats on her. He's told her, "If you ever try to leave, I'll get custody and you'll never get a dime from me or my family." Lorin's plan is long range—stay on good terms with her in-laws and get John into counseling. She hopes her in-laws will support the counseling, and she's even willing to go to marital counseling with John. Lorin has also developed a career plan so she'll be able to support herself and her older children if need be. Her mother-in-law is sympathetic, and will watch the kids while she goes to technical school to learn computer programming. In addition, because John has hit her only when she's confronted him about his affairs with other women, she decides not to bring them up any more as part of her protection plan for her and her children.

Leaving Strategies

A battered woman's safety strategies for leaving try to address batterer-generated and life-generated risks as she leaves or after she has left. A battered woman may plan to leave in a few days, a few years, or many years, so she may implement her safety strategies for leaving over short to long periods of time. If her plan to leave will take some time, then her protection and staying strategies will be long term and particularly significant. Long-range plans for leaving often illustrate both the resilience of battered women and the lack of true options available to them.

Whether a woman's safety strategy for leaving will be short or long term is determined by her risk analysis, personal and public resources, and the strategy itself. A safety plan for leaving for some women is simply walking out the door. For others, who may never have lived with their partner, it might mean ending the relationship, refusing to return calls, or refusing to see him. Long-range plans for leaving are often based on a particular occurrence in a battered woman's life. A woman might leave after she graduates from school, finds a job, receives a tax refund, her children finish school, or she meets someone new. Leaving a relationship may require some women to turn to the legal system. A safety plan for leaving, whether long range or short term, might include filing for divorce, seeking a custody order, trying to get support and health insurance for the children, and separating the couple's assets and liabilities. "Emergency"-type court actions might also be used, such as orders of protection or restraining orders. These actions may also deal with custody, visitation, contact with the woman, and who has the right to live where. Legal system involvement will add complexity to a battered woman's plans because she will be at the mercy of the system's response—often without an attorney to help her.

Because batterers frequently use the threat of a custody fight or child snatching to keep their partners from leaving, custody and visitation issues are a large part of most battered women's safety strategies for leaving. A battered woman may leave when she knows her partner will not get custody. She may wait until she can afford an attorney or one of the children is old enough to protect the younger children during visitation. Some battered women may wait to leave until their children reach an age when their opinion about where they want to live will be valued by the legal system.

Cira

Cira's risk analysis includes the risks to financial security for herself and her children and the physical violence of her husband. Her safety plan focuses on preserving her security. Her children are 12 and 14 and she wants them to be able to stay in the same home, schools, and neighborhood, and ultimately go to college. She has worked only part time in a job that doesn't pay well, and has no health benefits. Her husband's physical violence has been fairly minor until recently, when he was demoted at work and had his job changed to work he hates to do. Lately, when he comes home from work, he has started yelling, pushing, and shoving her in front of the children. She's worried that she or the kids may get hurt during one of these episodes and that they will start hating their father if it continues. Cira's safety plan includes protection strategies for herself and her children; she also has long-term strategies for staying and for leaving. Cira's protection strategy for her children is to feed them and send them to their room to do their homework before their father gets home from work, because this is the time when he is most likely to get violent. She has explained to them that their father is acting this way because of the stress of his job and that his behavior is not their fault. She also told them she'll be all right and doesn't need them to try to help her. Her plan includes talking with them and watching them closely; if she feels it's necessary, she'll take them to a therapist. Her staying strategy includes encouraging her husband to look for different work, work that he would enjoy more and would put less stress on him. He has responded to this suggestion and has contacted several employment agencies. In addition, Cira has started looking for full-time work with benefits for herself in case her husband loses his job completely or he takes a new job with less stress but also less money. Cira thinks if she has a full-time job, her husband might feel less pressure to be the breadwinner and, in the back of her mind, she thinks "If things don't get better, I'll be in a better position to leave."

Implications for Advocacy

Elements of Woman-Defined Advocacy

1. Understand the battered woman's perspective, including her risk analysis and safety plan.
   - Understand a battered woman's past and current safety plans.
   - ⅄ Identify staying, leaving, and protection strategies.
   - ⅄ Identify the time frame for a woman's current plans.

Fluidity of Safety Plans

Battered women's decision making and safety planning are fluid, part of an ongoing process to see risks, plan responses, try certain strategies, reevaluate, rethink, and try again. In other words, battered women change their minds. Change will depend on their hopes, their fears, the success or failure of their safety strategies, the response they get from the people they reach out to for help, and their partner's reaction. Battered women often talk about hope and fear when they talk about their relationships and their children. They often hope the violence will stop, their partners will change, and the children will be all right. Whether battered or not, women may hope that the love they have for their family will solve their problems. Hope is a powerful coping skill that sustains many women struggling with abusive partners. As battered women's hopes and fears change, their risk analyses and safety plans will change. When a woman's hope is high that her partner will change, her safety planning may focus on staying in the relationship. If she stays and her fear increases, then she may focus on leaving strategies. These shifts may take place over a significant period of time or in the course of a few minutes, hours, or days.

Two factors that have a significant effect on battered women's hope and fear are their partners and their advocates. A battered woman's partner may directly affect her hope and fear. If a woman's partner says he will change, stop getting angry and hitting her, and actually does change his behavior for some time, then the woman's hope may be high that things will be better and her plans will incorporate that belief. If, on the other hand, her partner reacts to a safety strategy by escalating his violence and control, then her fear will rise and her risk analysis and plans will incorporate her fear. For example, a woman tells her mother that her partner hits her. Her partner finds out, beats her, and threatens, "If you talk to anyone about me ever again—I'll kill you." This woman's fear will rise and the need to keep disclosures secret from her partner will become part of her analysis and planning.

Advocates can raise hope, lower fear, and then raise fear and lower hope all in a few minutes. For example, a battered woman calls the police because her partner beat her up. She goes to court and tells a victim advocate that she wants her husband ordered out of the home. The advocate tells her that is possible. The woman's hope is now high that her plan to keep him away from her will work. The advocate then starts to give the woman information about an education program that may help her partner control his anger. Despite the advocate's description of the program's limitations, the woman feels more hope that her partner will change, her fear of his violence lessens, and her plans shift to thinking about staying and not having him ordered out. The advocate next talks about what will happen to him if he does not go to the program: Some judges will do nothing and others might put him in jail for a day or so. The woman now considers whether her partner will go to the program and what might happen if he does not. She is worried that he might get very angry and physically hurt her in retaliation. Her fear rises, her hope for the success of this strategy fades, and her plans may change again.

Focus of Safety Plans

Battered women's safety plans may focus on a particular risk. A woman may focus on a risk because she believes she can successfully reduce it, someone told her to address it first, or she experiences it as the "worst." For example, if a woman experiences her partner's physical violence as tolerable, but living without sufficient financial resources as intolerable, then reducing the risk of losing financial resources will be the focus of her safety plan. A woman's perception of the consequences of pursuing a particular strategy will also influence her focus. An awareness that a battered woman has a reason for the particular focus will help an advocate understand the woman's risk analysis and planning.

Variety of Safety Plans

Advocates must be prepared to understand a wide variety of safety plans. Acknowledging that some battered women's plans do not focus on reducing physical violence and that others do not include leaving immediately as a viable strategy may require a shift in thinking for some advocates. In addition, some battered women's entire safety plan is built on their own personal support systems, and they may never use specialized family violence social, legal, or community services. For other women, these resources may be limited or nonexistent and the social service community will figure prominently in their plans.

What Information to Gather About
Battered Women's Safety Plans

Identifying a battered woman's current and past safety plans will add significantly to an advocate's understanding of her perspective. The history of past plans provides a sense of what strategies a woman has tried, what effect they had on her and the children, and how her partner reacted. They will also give advocates a sense of battered women's experiences with various helping systems and whether she would try them again. Along with an understanding of women's current strategies, a sense of past strategies will help guide advocates through resource and option identification, which we discuss further in Chapter 7, "Safety Planning with Battered Women."

Because battered women's safety plans can be very different, they will seek help for different reasons and with different goals. The reason a battered woman seeks help from a particular source can give advocates important information about her plan. For example, an individual battered woman may call the police for different reasons. A woman might call because she

- is afraid at the time she calls and wants the police to stop her partner from hurting her;
- wants the police to take her partner out of the home, either temporarily or permanently;
- wants her partner to know she is serious about her demands that he change;
- wants someone to make her partner stop hitting her;
- was told to call;
- wants to document the physical violence against her; or
- wants her partner to be punished for what he's done—perhaps have him put in jail.

Obviously, with such a variety of possible goals, how the police and the court system respond will have different effects on each woman's analysis and plans. This effect can be illustrated by looking at two examples. In the first, Linda calls the police because she is afraid her partner is going to hurt her at the time she calls; in the second, Tracy calls because she wants her partner to change.

Linda

Linda's goals are short term. She hasn't necessarily thought through the possible ramifications of police involvement; she is simply trying to survive a violent attack. If the police are able to respond in time—before she is seriously hurt—and they find probable cause to arrest her partner and take him into custody, then her goal of surviving the attack will have been met. Linda's outreach to the police is "successful"—they get there before she is seriously injured. Once her partner is arrested, then the court system will also respond in some way. Because Linda's goal in calling the police is to survive this attack, she may have to think about and define her goals for the court's response. How she defines her goals and how the court responds may affect whether she will call the police again. Linda knows from this experience, however, that if she is in physical danger from her partner, she can call the police and their response may be in time to interrupt the violence.

Tracy

Tracy's goal in calling the police is to let her partner know she is serious when she says she won't tolerate his violence and wants him to get some help. She's tried talking to him, but this hasn't worked—he's hit her again. She calls the police. The police respond and say, "If we make any arrest, we'll have to take you both in." Tracy has successfully demonstrated her seriousness by calling the police. The police response, however, undermines her goal of getting her partner to understand that he needs to change. By threatening to arrest both Tracy and her partner, the police give her partner the message that they are both responsible for his hitting her, and that there will be no consequences for his behavior. Because there is no arrest, there will be no opportunity for the court to respond.

If a response increases a battered woman's danger or creates new risks, then the response itself may not be safe. For example, a battered woman might apply for an order of protection and end up having to fight for, and perhaps ultimately lose custody of, her children. A battered woman may call the police to stop her partner from hitting her and she may be arrested. A few visits to a therapist or battered woman's counselor may result in a report to child protective services, who remove the battered woman's children. A return call from a lawyer is recorded on a caller identification unit and results in interrogation and retribution from her abusive partner. A call regarding a job training program may lead to deportation or other immigration problems. A call to the school regarding her children may lead to a school official calling her partner, the children's father, and disclosing her location. If the response itself endangers the woman and adds new risks for her, she is unlikely to include it in her safety plans.

Summary: Information to Gather About Safety Plans

- Identify past safety plans
  - What has she tried?
  - How did it work?
  - Would she try it again? If not, why not?
  - What was her partner's reaction?
- Identify current safety plans, including protection, staying, and leaving strategies
  - What is the time frame for her strategies?
  - What personal and public resources has she identified?
  - How does she think her partner will react to her strategies?

Note

1. The literature on the divorce process provides ample evidence of the difficulties and complexities often involved in terminating relationships, even without the complexities of physical abuse. See, for example, Salts (1979) and Wiseman (1975). Kurz (1996) analyzes the role of violence in ending the marriage and the added problems it brings to women's postdivorce experience.

P A R T   I I

BUILDING PARTNERSHIPS WITH BATTERED WOMEN

Woman-defined advocacy seeks to build a partnership between the advocate and the battered woman—a partnership in which both the woman's and the advocate's perspectives, information, and knowledge are shared, and ultimately the best safety plan is formed and implemented. Although the advocacy will be defined by the battered woman, the advocate is an active participant in the partnership.

Woman-defined advocacy has two primary components: First, advocates must understand the woman's perspective; second, advocates must integrate their own knowledge, resources, and advocacy into the woman's analysis and plans. This integration includes a review of the battered woman's analysis and plans, which is discussed in Chapter 6, "Risk Analysis." Strengthening the woman's existing safety plans is explored in Chapter 7, "Safety Planning With Battered Women."

6

Risk Analysis

Safety plans seek to reduce certain risks. Therefore, a thorough and accurate risk analysis is an essential component of safety planning. To ensure that a battered woman's analysis is as complete as it can be, an advocate can review the analysis with her. This chapter discusses risk analysis review in general and two primary risks in detail: specifically, lethality or life-threatening violence and risks to children. The last section provides guidance on how to approach the review for all women and for women whose risk analysis appears extremely inaccurate. This chapter ends with a discussion of some of the personal challenges advocates may face in completing a review.

The purpose of reviewing a battered woman's risk analysis is to ensure that both the advocate and the battered woman have the best possible information about the risks the woman and her children face. A review means an advocate thinks about the risks the woman has described, checks for any miscommunication or misunderstanding, and factors in the advocate's own analysis. Reviewing a battered woman's risk analysis requires a delicate balance of adding to and enhancing the information a woman has without completely replacing her judgment with that of the advocate. For example, a battered woman tells an advocate that her only concern is being evicted from her home because her boyfriend forced her to give him her paycheck and spent the rent money on cocaine. An advocate would start a review of the woman's risk analysis by validating her concern about eviction, then exploring what "force" was used to get the paycheck. The advocate would also explore the potential risks the woman might face because of her boyfriend's cocaine use. The review respectfully combines the battered woman's information, experience, and priorities with the advocate's knowledge and understanding.

A review has three components. One is the range of risks that each individual woman faces, both directly from her partner's abusive actions—batterer-generated risks—and the other life-generated risks or concerns she may have. The second is the woman's perception of how staying in or trying to leave the relationship will affect those risks. Does she think leaving will make a risk greater? The third component is the meaning a woman assigns to the risks she and her children face. Different women may assign different meanings to the same risk. How a battered woman views her risks and how an advocate responds to this view will affect every aspect of advocacy: what she will tell an advocate, whether she thinks the advocate can help, whether she thinks a particular response will be helpful, and whether she will consider the information the advocate provides. When an advocate reviews a battered woman's risk analysis, lethal or life-threatening violence and risks to children are two areas of particular concern.

Review of Life-Threatening Risks

Predicting human behavior is difficult; this includes predicting which batterers will kill or try to kill their partners. The review of life-threatening violence against a battered woman, as with all risks, should begin with the woman's view. Most battered women are not killed, but the potential for life-threatening violence should be explored with every woman. In many situations, it will be impossible to determine if the advocate's analysis of life-threatening violence is any better than the battered woman's. Battered women constantly assess and respond to the physical violence and other controlling tactics of their partners, including life-threatening violence. Life-threatening violence may be directed solely at the woman, at the woman and her children, or perhaps at only the children. Advocates should err on the side of caution, while remembering that not all battered women are in extreme danger. In practice, this can be a difficult balance. Once the potential for life-threatening violence is identified for either the mother or the children, *enhanced advocacy,* as discussed in Chapter 7, "Safety Planning With Battered Women," must begin.

One of the reasons it is so difficult to predict which batterers are most likely to kill their partners is because, relatively speaking, they do it so rarely. It is much easier to predict something that happens frequently. In fact, researchers have tried for many years to develop models that can predict any kind of violence, and they have had limited success. In general, they have found that a past history of violence is the best predictor. They have also found that alcoholics or chronic alcohol users have 12 times higher rates of violence than nonusers, and that drug users have violence rates 16 times higher than nonusers of drugs or alcohol (Limandri & Sheridan, 1995). Researchers have also found that people who have particularly serious psychiatric diagnoses (such as schizophrenia, major depression, and bipolar disorders) are five times more likely to use violence than people who do not meet the criteria for these diagnoses. This does not mean that people with serious psychiatric disorders are necessarily violent, or even that most of them are. It means simply that they have been found to be more likely to use violence than other people, for whatever reason.

Despite the relative infrequency, more than 1,500 women over the age of 10 were killed by their husband, ex-husband, or boyfriend in the United States in 1993 (Federal Bureau of Investigation, 1993), and that rate has remained fairly stable over the past 15 years. African American women were killed by intimates at higher rates than Caucasian women. Women were most likely to be killed with a gun: a woman's risk of being killed by a partner is nearly eight times higher if there is a gun in the home (Kellermann et al., 1993). The women who were killed were also likely to have a history of physical abuse: Approximately two thirds were abused before they were killed (Campbell, 1992).

Researchers do not yet have clear answers to questions about the factors that can accurately predict when a woman is likely to be killed by her partner. Campbell (1995b) developed the Danger Assessment to be used in hospital, shelters, and other settings in an effort to learn more. In the meantime, the majority of a group of experts agreed on nine risk factors: access to or ownership of guns; use of a weapon in past incidents; threats with weapons; threats to kill; serious injury in past incidents; threats of suicide; drug or alcohol abuse; forced sex; and obsessiveness or extreme jealousy or dominance (Campbell, 1995b). Of course, none of these factors, nor any combination of them, is a certain predictor.

Probably the most important indication of life-threatening violence is the woman's perception of her danger. If the woman is very afraid and says she will be killed or may be killed, then the possibility of life-threatening violence is present. As Barbara Hart (1988) notes, "Battered women are usually the best evaluators of the potential for lethal violence because they generally have more information about the batterer than anyone other than the batterer himself" (p. 240). Right now, it appears that the best approach to screening for life-threatening violence is a combination of the woman's perspective and the advocate's assessment.

The following discussion on screening for life-threatening violence is based on a variety of sources, including numerous discussions with advocates and women who have survived serious assaults. It is essential to remember that even when there is a risk of extreme violence, the woman's perspective and understanding of her risk still need to be the starting place for advocacy. If she says, "He's going to kill me," believe her. Even when a woman seems unconcerned about extreme violence but the advocate is very afraid for her, the advocate still needs to start with the battered woman's perspective of her risk.

As stated earlier, there are no conclusive studies that show which batterers will actually kill or seriously injure their partners or children. It seems that a gut feeling brought on by certain combinations of factors or circumstances is the most common screening tool used and may sometimes be an accurate indicator of life-threatening violence. As screening tools for life-threatening violence are developed and research is conducted to indicate if they are accurate, then advocacy should incorporate these tools. Although an advocate cannot always predict accurately which batterers will kill, and ultimately the woman has the right and responsibility to make decisions for herself, it is the advocate's role to provide a battered woman with information that she may not have so the woman can include it in her risk analysis.

The following list does not provide a way to distinguish lethal from nonlethal situations. It is simply meant to give advocates a sense of the range of factors that might indicate lethal situations and therefore need further exploration and enhanced advocacy. Some of the following factors or circumstances were collected by Susan Schechter (1982) and identified by battered women and advocates as useful when considering the risk of extreme violence.

- Batterer history
  - Previous assaults against her
  - Previous assaults against others
  - Suicide attempts or threats
  - Homicide threats or attempts
  - Homicidal fantasies
  - Prior use or threats with weapons
  - His own childhood of victimization or witnessing abuse of his mother

- Batterer behavior
  - Drug and alcohol abuse
  - Monitoring and stalking
  - Terrorizing or sadistic behaviors
  - Escalating frequency or severity of aggressiveness
  - Terrorizing and sadistic sexual abuse or humiliation
  - Threatening with weapons
  - Physical and sexual abuse of the children
  - Abuse of her during pregnancy

- Batterer personality
  - Paranoid, jealous
  - Emotional disregard of others or lack of empathy; coldness or cruelty
  - Serious depression
  - Insecure, desperate, dependent
  - Entitled or possessive: "If I can't have her, nobody will"

- Context
  - Separation
  - Availability of weapons
  - Losses: job, deaths, illness
  - Exposure of victim's or offender's secrets—affairs, illegal activity, incest
  - Victim's use of weapons
  - Victim's escalating use of violence
  - Victim's suicide attempts
  - Institutional rejections of her search for help (failed attempts at safety)
  - Victim's abuse of substances

In addition to these factors, advocates should identify and list other elements they consider when trying to identify extreme danger.

- A victim saying, "He gives me the creeps" or he's gone "crazy" or "He just has that look in his eyes" or "He's just not the same, he's changed, he doesn't care about anything" or "He was crazier than usual. He never threatened to kill me before."
- Vietnam veteran with flashbacks
- Martial arts, military, police officer (training, access to weapons)
- Sudden change in abuser's behavior
- Violence toward pets
- Obsession with violent pornography
- The batterer starts to attack the woman outside the house
- The batterer violates protective orders or restraining orders

- The abuser increases the woman's isolation
- The abuser forces the woman to do drugs

It is important to remember that these factors are only associated with increased risk and do not necessarily indicate which batterers will kill. For example, most battered women in households with a gun are not killed, just as most women who have been abused are not ultimately killed. So, if an individual battered woman tells an advocate that there is a gun in the house, it does not mean she will be killed, it simply means she may be at increased risk.

Review of Risks for Children

Advocacy for battered women must include the children within their care, because the children must be protected. Once again, understanding a battered woman's risk analysis for her children is the starting point for a review. Concerns about children often figure prominently for battered women because of their genuine concern for and commitment to the children, and because batterers frequently use threats or actions about the children to continue their control. Battered mothers' risk analyses for their children may include a range of concerns, such as physical violence, the children's financial security, their emotional security, and their future well-being. Battered mothers may worry about the effects of growing up in a "broken home" or without a father in the home, or living in poverty. The "stay/leave" factor will also affect battered mothers' analyses of their children's risks.

Protecting children from being hit and from the effects of witnessing domestic violence is justified and compelling. Yet, like a battered mother, a child's risks are not limited to physical violence and its effects. The battered mother's risk analysis will provide information about both the child's risks and the mother's risks and decision making. If the mother's decision making is faulty and does not adequately address the children's risks, the advocate may have to take action to protect the children. When significant risks for children are identified, enhanced advocacy is called for. Mothers leaving their relationship will not necessarily remove the risks for the children, and for some children, leaving may even increase their risks.

Although most battered women carefully and accurately analyze the risks to their children, some battered women do not, some women's analyses are incomplete or inaccurate, and some battered women are a threat to their children. As we showed in Chapter 3, "Batterer-Generated Risks," physical abuse of children is common in households where the mother is being beaten. For example, in Bowker et al.'s (1988) study, the batterer abused both the mother and the children in 70% of the cases in which there were children in the household. The children were more likely to be abused when the battering was worse (it was more frequent, more severe, and more frequently included rape) and when there were larger numbers of children. Research still cannot tell us definitively which men who batter women are also most likely to abuse their children, however.

Studies have found that battered women sometimes abuse their children as well, although they do so at significantly lower rates than battering men do. For example, Stark and Flitcraft (1988) found that half of the batterers also abused the children, compared to 35% of the battered women. Straus (1983) reports that his first national survey found that batterers were twice as likely as battered women to abuse their children more than two times a year. Battered women were twice as likely as nonbattered women to abuse their children more than two times a year.

Although women often make decisions about safety and the future of their relationship based on their concerns about their children, systematic data on women's perceptions of their children's risks have not been collected. Studies do suggest that as the abuse women experience becomes more frequent and severe, more of women's energy becomes focused on their own survival. Unfortunately, these are precisely the circumstances when children are more likely to be abused, as well. This means that the worse the woman's abuse, the more concerns and questions the advocates should have about any children in the household.

Review of risks to children is complex and requires a thorough understanding of the battered mother's risk analysis. In reviewing mothers' analyses for their children, the advocate must distinguish among mothers who have little or no options and therefore have taken little action to address their children's risks, mothers who have tried to take action but have not successfully reduced the risk, and mothers who have not tried to respond at all. The distinction will help determine when advocates must take action unilaterally—without the mother's involvement—to protect the children. Unilateral action typically means making a report to state child protective services. When reports must be made to child protective services, advocates have urged that interventions be planned and coordinated so that women are not inaccurately blamed or their relationships with their children jeopardized and that women's safety needs are considered as child protection service workers interview family members and plan services. As Peled (1996) notes:

> Child protective services should support and collaborate with the efforts of battered women's advocates to protect battered women and their children from further abuse. The perpetrator of violence must be held accountable not only for the abuse of his partner but also for the emotional abuse of the witnessing children. (p. 135)

Figure 6.1 summarizes several types of battered mothers' risk analyses and plans for their children and the suggested advocate responses, including when unilateral action is necessary.

Implications for Advocacy

How to Approach the Review of Risk Analysis

As with all aspects of advocacy with battered women, the review must be done with humility, honesty, and respect. Humility means knowing your limitations by having a thorough understanding of both your strengths and your weaknesses. Advocacy requires the humility to accept the limitations of your response fully. The advocate's specific role, and the system in which he or she advocates, can impose various constraints. In addition, all advocates have the following limitations: 1) advocates cannot predict what every batterer will do; 2) advocates cannot guarantee that all women and their children will be safe; 3) there is a lot advocates do not understand about family violence or its effects on women or children; 4) there is a lot advocates do not know about responses to family violence and their effects on batterers, women, or children; 5) analysis and advocacy are hindered if advocates are unable to obtain accurate and thorough information from the woman (and this may be significantly limited due to time or other constraints); 6) everyone has life experience, background, and training that lead to biases and gaps in understanding; and 7) no one can know everything about every risk or reduce every risk.

Honesty means carefully conveying these limitations to the battered woman, stating clearly when the advocate is simply suggesting possibilities and when he or she actually knows something for sure. Respect includes being slow to differ with the woman's analysis and, when there is a difference, to convey that information with sensitivity.

Battered Mother's Risk Analysis	Advocate Response
Accurately identifies no batterer-generated risks to the children.	Focus on advocacy for the battered mother.
Identifies risks to the children, and her safety plan successfully reduces those risks.	Focus on advocacy for the battered mother.
Identifies risks to the children, but has few or no options available to reduce those risks or those options are unsuccessful.	Work with the mother to try to reduce risks to the children.
Identifies risks to the children, but she has no real options because of her partner's physical violence.	Work with the mother to reduce the risk of physical violence to her as part of the advocacy to reduce risks to the children.
Does not identify risks to the children because she is unaware of the effects on them.	Review her risk analysis with her. If she then understands the risks, work with her to try to reduce them. If she doesn't see the risks, take unilateral action to protect the children.
Does not identify risks because she is not committed to parenting or protecting the children.	Take unilateral action to protect the children.
Does not identify risks because she is abusing the children.	Review her risk analysis with her. If she wants to reduce them determine what immediate steps she needs to take. If not, take unilateral action to protect the children.

Figure 6.1. Considerations for Action by Advocates to Respond to Children's Risks

Challenges to Understanding the Battered Woman's Risk Analysis and Plans

Understanding a battered woman's risk analysis presents an advocate with a number of challenges. An initial challenge is understanding that some battered women do not see physical violence as their primary risk or leaving as their most viable option. Accepting this reality will be a shift for some advocates because much of the response to domestic violence assumes that battered women's greatest concerns are their partners' physical violence and that leaving will reduce that risk. This focus comes from not only a genuine desire to protect battered women and children, but also a limited view of batterer-generated and life-generated risks. The result is an almost exclusive reliance on safety strategies for leaving. Most advocates have considerable experience working with women who do not want to leave, or who have left and gone back to their partners, but may have limited experience working with women to enhance their safety plans for staying. Working with battered women whose plans are to stay in the relationship may challenge advocates to develop new ways of thinking about how they do their work and how they define success. It may also mean developing and integrating new resources, contacts, and options for women.

Advocates and battered women may have different information and goals when they meet for the first time. Advocates may have a lot of information about the services, systems, and options available to battered women. A battered woman may have little information about those resources, but a great deal of information about the risks she faces, her partner, what options have worked or failed in the past, what personal resources she has, and how her children are doing. Advocates must communicate effectively with women to understand their perspectives and enhance their safety plans. As advocates gather and interpret information, other challenges arise.

What information a battered woman actually provides to an advocate will be influenced by the interaction with the advocate and the woman's own ability to assess and communicate her perspective. If a battered woman does not trust an advocate, think the advocate will be helpful, or believe the advocate will be sympathetic, the woman may communicate a story that does not accurately reflect her risk analysis and plans. Whatever the cause, an inaccurate understanding of a battered woman's perspective will significantly limit an advocate's ability to enhance a battered woman's safety plans.

Sal—A Battered Woman's Advocate

Cindy has been forced into prostitution by her batterer and believes that Sal, her advocate, will not help her if she finds out she's a prostitute. So Cindy doesn't tell Sal about her risk analysis of the prostitution, including her fears of getting HIV, getting beaten up by a john, being arrested, and having her children taken away by child protection services. This produces a significant gap in Sal's view of Cindy's risks. This gap may lead to confusing or contradictory goals as Sal works with Cindy to enhance her safety plans. Cindy's existing plan does not include calling the police because Cindy's partner told her the police would recognize her and they'd never believe a prostitute. Because Sal doesn't know all Cindy's risk analysis, she may not understand why Cindy won't call the police and may begin to make negative judgments about her and her plans. These judgments might include, "She won't help herself"; "I told her to call the police, but she doesn't listen"; "She's minimizing and denying the danger she's in"; "She's protecting him because she's co-dependent and helpless." In addition, Sal's incomplete picture of Cindy's risks will keep her from assisting in Sal's safety plans for those risks, including information about HIV transmission, child protective services responses, and ways to protect herself from the johns.

Sometimes an advocate may believe that a particular battered woman's analysis or plans are not in the woman's best interest. This can make it extremely difficult for the advocate to build on the woman's plans, particularly if the risk of physical violence may be life-threatening. Woman-defined advocacy does not preclude advocates from providing different perspectives to the woman, particularly if a review of the woman's analysis identifies the potential for life-threatening violence. Reviewing a battered woman's risk analysis does not mean replacing her decision making, however. If the advocate goes too far, it is not the woman who is defining the advocacy, but the advocate.

Dana—A Battered Woman's Advocate

Carla's husband, Ron, is extremely controlling. Ron is a police officer. He tracks Carla's every move, doesn't allow her to drive, and gives her only enough money to buy food. Ron slaps Carla once in awhile, but hasn't done anything more. Recently, Ron has been very down and agitated, often talking about suicide. Last week, a neighbor called to complain about their dog's barking. Ron got very upset and went in the backyard and shot the dog. Ron and Carla's two children were very upset and told their teacher. The teacher called Carla and suggested she call the local domestic violence project.

Dana, an advocate from the project, listens to Carla's story. Carla's risk analysis includes concerns that Ron will lose his job if he remains so down and that he would never really do anything to physically hurt her or the children. Carla's plan is to talk with Ron's superior officer at work, who is a good friend of Ron's and has always been sympathetic to Carla. She believes Ron will get the help he needs through the police union. Dana dismisses Carla's plan by not commenting on it at all and concludes that Ron is going to kill Carla. Dana tells Carla that if she doesn't go to the shelter, Ron will kill her.

Dana—not Carla—is defining the advocacy. If Dana used a more woman-defined approach, she would begin by validating Carla's analysis and plan. She would tell Carla she believes she is in danger, and explain why. She would provide information about the shelter and other protection strategies without deciding what is best for Carla. Dana would speak to Carla frequently to see if the circumstances are changing.

An advocate's own life experience, background, and training will guide how he or she interprets information battered women provide. This can be both a strength and a challenge. It is a strength when it helps the advocate understand the battered woman's perspective and a challenge when an advocate's perspective and emotions interfere with the ability to "hear" what the woman is saying.

Tina—A Battered Woman's Advocate

Tina is working with Alice. Tina is a recovering alcoholic and feels very strongly that women have to stop drinking before they can fix other things in their lives. Alice wants Tina to help her get a protective order against her boyfriend. During their conversation, Alice mentions that she sometimes drinks to dull her fear. Tina tells Alice that she is an alcoholic. Alice says to Tina,

"You're overreacting. I just have a few drinks." Tina becomes extremely angry at Alice for "denying she has a problem." Tina never talks with Alice about getting a protective order.

When an advocate's experience gets mixed in with the battered woman's in such a negative way, it can make interactions difficult and advocacy ineffective. This mixing is a normal part of human interaction, but when it keeps advocates from understanding and sympathizing with battered women, it must be identified and addressed. Clinicians refer to this phenomenon as *countertransference*. Addressing it starts by identifying when an advocate is having very strong feelings toward a woman, particularly anger. Then the advocate should check out the strong feelings with a colleague, supervisor, or trained clinical supervisor. Skilled supervision can help advocates keep their "own stuff" from getting in the way of helping battered women.

Throughout this book, we have encouraged advocates to be honest, humble, and respectful when working with battered women. This is especially important when advocates explore and respond to personal biases. The challenge for an advocate is to identify when race, ethnicity, sexual orientation, gender, age, or class biases are keeping him or her from understanding a battered woman's perspective or supporting the woman's decisions and plans.

Joan—A Shelter Advocate

Nina has just told Joan she has found a place to stay with her three children and will be leaving the shelter this afternoon. Joan asks about the place and Nina tells her it is a small house with two bedrooms. Nina hopes eventually to have enough money to be able to have the electricity turned on. Joan tells Nina she thinks the house is an inappropriate and unsafe environment to raise three children because it has only two bedrooms and no electricity. Nina tells Joan the house is better than the shelter and also better than the home she and her children lived in when they were in Puerto Rico.

Joan's interpretation and evaluation of Nina's safety plan is skewed by a class and perhaps also a racial or ethnic bias. Joan's approach is not woman defined, will not enhance Nina's safety plans, and may keep Nina from seeking help from the shelter again.

Advocates work with battered women who have different perspectives, races, cultures, abilities, dangers, and demands. Bias and ignorance prevent effective advocacy. Understanding a battered woman's perspective requires a commitment by advocates to grasp—and respond supportively to—the effect race, class, ethnicity, age, ability, sexual orientation, and religion may have on a woman's analysis and plans. One way to check for biases is to make a conscious effort to assess interactions with battered women. Ongoing support and supervision from colleagues or supervisors can also help keep personal biases from hindering advocacy. Perhaps the most important strategy is for advocates to remain open to reconsidering and changing their point of view. Self-awareness and a commitment to respecting battered women's uniqueness and diversity are essential.

Review When the Woman's Analysis
Appears Extremely Inaccurate or Incomplete

This section discusses situations in which the woman's analysis is extremely inaccurate or incomplete, not just analyses that are missing some information or based on inaccurate assumptions. For example, a battered woman's risk analysis is that a creature that lives in the tire of her car has taken over her family and influences anyone who tries to intervene. She tells the advocate she knows this because "the tire speaks to me and tells me things." The woman also tells the advocate she cannot trust her, because the tire told her he controls what the advocate does. This is an extreme example. This woman's analysis is inaccurate and indicates mental health issues.

As discussed in Chapter 4, "Life-Generated Risks," some battered women have mental health issues that affect their judgment and their ability to function effectively. In some cases, the women had these issues before they experienced battering by their partners. Women who have serious mental health problems may be at greater risk of abuse than others. In other cases, the mental health issues may have been caused by the abuse they have suffered from their partner over time. Studies have found that women who have experienced chronic and severe violence, especially physical abuse combined with repeated sexual violence, are most likely to have the most pronounced emotional reactions (e.g., Dutton, 1992; Shields & Hanneke, 1983; Walker, 1984). For some women, these reactions can include loss of memory of episodes of serious abuse and what psychologists call *emotional numbing,* constricted affect, hypervigilance, intrusive flashbacks, and denial and avoidance. These are also among the features of posttraumatic stress disorder (PTSD), which some researchers have found in varying degrees among some samples of battered women. Most of these samples have come from battered women who have sought refuge in shelters.

It can be difficult to identify whether mental health issues are making a woman's analysis inaccurate. For example, a battered woman with mental health issues may continue to tell one aspect of her story over and over again. Although repetitive, the story may correctly reflect the woman's perspective and the advocate would be able to develop an accurate view of this woman's analysis and plans. As part of the review process, it is important for an advocate to know his or her own limits. An advocate who might be skilled in crisis intervention may not have the skill to determine the accuracy of a battered woman's perspective when she also has delusions. The advocate should work with the woman, but seek support and guidance from mental health professionals about what advocacy role she can play. The advocate should offer the woman information and referrals to resources in the community that will respond appropriately to her mental health issues. When a woman's analysis appears "way off," however, the advocate should not assume that the woman has a mental health issue; instead, the first consideration should be to find out why the analysis appears inaccurate. The woman's analysis may appear inaccurate or incomplete because the woman is not conveying her real analysis or because it *is* extremely inaccurate or incomplete. This is an important distinction. Another explanation for disparate analysis is that the advocate's analysis is inaccurate or incomplete.

A battered woman may have a good reason not to convey her analysis accurately. In fact, if she believes disclosing her analysis will make things worse for her or her children, then hiding it may be part of her safety plans. For example, she may keep secret her or her partner's illegal activity, such as drugs or prostitution. She might not tell the entire story because she is afraid of losing her children, or afraid of being judged because she is immoral or thinks she deserves so little. In these circumstances, advocates might focus on trying to figure out what the woman thinks will happen if she talks candidly— what would be "made worse." Then, if it is possible for the advocate to allay that fear, the woman may speak freely.

If the battered woman's analysis is extremely inaccurate, and if the inaccuracy is caused by mental health issues, then identifying and responding to the issue must be part of advocacy. Depending on the expertise of the advocate, this might mean direct intervention or a referral. Battered women with mental health issues face the same risks as other battered women. The types of mental health issues can vary widely and will have different effects on the woman's analysis and interaction with the advocate. A battered woman may have a mental disability and an accurate risk analysis. Advocates must not make assumptions about a particular woman's abilities, but at the same time, they must be aware of a woman's functional limitations to provide a review that will be useful to her analysis.

Elements of Woman-Defined Advocacy

2. Build a partnership with a battered woman.
   □ Respectfully review a battered woman's risk analysis.
   ▲ Review life-threatening violence.
   ▲ Review risks to children.

The review must be done respectfully and carefully to ensure that the woman and the advocate are getting the best analysis possible. A review should begin with the battered woman's analysis and the assumption that the analysis is accurate. A parallel assumption is that the advocate will provide additional, significant information that may enhance the woman's overall analysis and planning. For example, if a woman's strategy raises additional risks (e.g., she drinks heavily to numb the pain and anxiety), then the advocate's review would include the potential pitfalls of alcohol as a coping strategy. This review will be successful only if the battered woman trusts the advocate enough to hear what he or she is saying.

Lethality

If the advocate identifies any factor that leads him or her to believe lethality is an issue, the advocate should explore further to identify the woman's perspective regarding lethality and any additional factors. Consider asking questions such as:

- What do you think he might do?
- Do you think he's capable of carrying out his threat to [fill in the blank]?
- Tell me about him. What's he like when he's really scary/angry?

- What is the scariest thing he has done?

Children

To review risks for children of battered mothers, advocates need to understand the mother's perception of the risks, and identify risks the mother may not include in her analysis. Consider asking such questions as:

- What is it like in your home when your partner is angry?
- Do you talk to the children about it? What do you tell them? What do they say about it?
- What do the children do when it happens?
- Have they tried to help, to intervene?
- Have they been injured? How? Describe the injuries.
- Do you think they have been affected by your partner's anger? How?
- Have you noticed any change in their behavior, school performance, and the like?

Proceed carefully when taking unilateral action to protect the children (see Figure 6.1).

- Fully understand the mother's risk analysis and safety plans for her children before taking action. Consider if the analysis is accurate.
- Try to work with the mother whenever possible.
- Notify and involve the mother when you take unilateral action, if it will not further endanger the children.
- If you do take unilateral action, tell the mother what you will or will not be able to do to help her. Try to find a way to help her. Make appropriate referrals for her.

Conveying a Different Analysis

If the advocate's analysis is different from the battered woman's, the advocate should consider the following when conveying that perspective.

1. Clarify the woman's analysis to ensure that there is truly a difference and not just a miscommunication.
2. Consider the timing of the review.
   - Does it all need to be done in this interaction? Will you have contact with the woman over a period of time and have the opportunity to complete the review in pieces?

      ▫ Are there parts of the review, such as life-threatening violence or risks to the children, that should get priority?

3. Be observant.

      ▫ How is the woman reacting to this additional or differing information? What is her body language? Her demeanor? Ask her how the review is affecting her.

      ▫ Is the review destroying any trust she may have developed? What are the implications for this? Does she understand what you're trying to tell her?

4. Consider the circumstances of the interaction.

      ▫ Is the conversation in person or over the telephone?

      ▫ Is the woman speaking voluntarily or is there some requirement or pressure on her to talk?

      ▫ Is the conversation private?

5. Be cautious about using outside information in the review.

      ▫ Have you had the opportunity to check its accuracy and thoroughness?

      ▫ How will the woman react when she knows you have it? Will she think you believe the outsider more than her?

7

Safety Planning With Battered Women

Elements of Woman-Defined Advocacy

2. Build a partnership with a battered woman.
   □ Work with a battered woman to strengthen her safety plan.
   ⅄ Identify available and relevant options and resources.
   ⅄ Analyze these options with the battered woman.
   ⅄ Develop and implement the refined safety plan.
   ⅄ Provide enhanced advocacy when needed, and in all cases of life-threatening violence.

Woman-defined advocacy seeks to work with each battered woman to ensure she has the best safety plan possible. Although battered women do their own safety planning, advocates can often provide women with information and analysis that will result in more complete safety plans. This chapter discusses three components of an approach to enhance and implement safety plans with battered women: 1) identify available and relevant options, 2) analyze options (not previously reviewed) with the battered woman, and 3) develop an implementation strategy—a safety plan.

Identify Available and Relevant Options and Resources

For advocates to identify available and relevant options and resources, they must have advanced knowledge of the potential option to know if it is truly available to a particular battered woman.

113

Advocates must also incorporate the individual woman's analysis, plans, and resources to ensure that the option is relevant. Agencies often have conditions or requirements that women have to meet before the option is available to them. When advocates identify potential options, they must be aware of and convey these conditions. For example, there may be income or geographic eligibility requirements; a requirement that a woman has—or does not have—a particular type of issue, such as substance abuse; or requirements that a woman has already left her partner or her children are of a certain age or gender, she can come into the office for help, she is a U.S. citizen, or she speaks English. Any one of these conditions could be a barrier for an individual battered woman. If the barrier prevents the woman from using the option, it is not an available option for her.

Options can come from three sources: the advocate, the battered woman, or another agency or system. When the advocate is the source, the advocate provides the options or facilitates their use. For example, the advocate may provide counseling or access to shelter. The battered woman herself may have significant options or resources available to her. For example, she may have money, friends, family, clergy, or her employer's support. If she needs housing, she can move. If she needs someone to talk with, she can turn to a family member or friend. If she needs someone to help protect her children, she can have a relative move in with her. If she wants to get a court order to keep her partner away, she can hire an attorney to help her. Any woman may have few or none of these options. Then resources from the advocate or other agency or system may be the only ones available. Other agencies or systems might include the legal system, agencies that provide mental health or substance abuse services, agencies that administer government benefits, health care providers, and housing advocacy groups.

Select the Options That Respond to the
Woman's Risk Analysis After the Review

If the advocate provides new or additional risk information during the review, the advocate must determine whether the woman has incorporated that information into her analysis. New or additional information might change the woman's analysis immediately or at a later date, or not affect it at all. If the advocate's risk analysis is different from the woman's, and the advocate does not realize that the review did little to bring them closer, then the advocate may identify options or resources relevant to the advocate's analysis but not to the woman's. If the analyses remain different, the advocate could begin by presenting options relevant to the woman's analysis. The advocate may also want to provide information about options relevant to the advocate's own analysis, particularly if they are protection strategies for the woman or her children. The advocate would do so in all cases where the analysis indicates the possibility of life-threatening violence.

Relevant options and resources respond to the reviewed risk analysis and build on a woman's present safety plans. For example, if the woman's risk analysis is that she and her children are primarily in danger of losing the necessities of life if her partner loses his job, then options that will allow him to keep his job will be relevant. These might include evening counseling or weekend incarceration, but not a continuous prison sentence.

If the woman's plan is to leave the state at the end of the month and move in with her family, then local resources that require her long-term involvement will not be relevant.

If the woman's plan is to live with her partner until she finishes school and gets a job, then resources that focus on her separating from him now will not be relevant. Resources that help her to complete school will further her plan.

If the woman's plan is to leave with the intention of returning—to let him know that she is seriously considering leaving him if he does not stop his violence—then resources that focus on leaving permanently will not be relevant.

Determine if the Woman Can Meet the Requirements for Using the Option

For example, a woman may tell an advocate that her ex-husband has been stalking her. Her risk analysis is that he probably will not hurt her, he just wants to frighten her and find out if she is dating someone new. She thinks that a court order might scare him and make him stop. She does not know where he lives or works, however, and has no way of contacting him. Therefore, she cannot provide "service" (legal notification of a restraining order), and the judge in her state will not order a court order if there is no service. This option is not available to this woman.

Analyze These Options With the Battered Woman

Analyzing options with a battered woman, like reviewing her risk analysis, provides both the advocate and the battered woman with an opportunity to get the best possible information. Information about available options includes how options might affect the woman's and children's lives, plans, and safety. For example, a woman may be planning to support herself, leave her husband, and serve him with divorce papers. She is worried about his reaction when he gets the papers. The advocate suggests that the battered woman go to a shelter until the husband gets the papers and she determines his reaction. The shelter is 100 miles from her job, however, and she cannot take any time off from work. Therefore, staying at the shelter would not further her plan, and other alternatives would need to be explored, such as staying at a friend's house.

Describe the Options

Jargon is frequently used to describe options. If the woman does not understand the jargon, she will not be able to consider the option or use it effectively in her plans. Part of the description should include how the options will proceed, such as the steps involved, the usual timetable, the roles of people involved, decisions that will be needed along the way, and what influence, if any, the woman can have. For example, the advocate may describe calling the police as an option. The battered woman can decide whether or not to call the police. Once the police are called, however, they will decide how to respond. If they decide to make an arrest, then a prosecutor will make decisions about how the case proceeds in court. The battered woman may or may not have the opportunity to influence decisions about the arrest or prosecution of her partner.

Explore the Consequences of Pursuing or Not Pursuing a Particular Option

This means trying to anticipate what will happen. Will the option further the woman's safety plans or will it make things worse? Will pursuing the option create additional risks? Sometimes advocates will not be able to predict the likely outcome, and that also would be important to convey to the woman.

Explore Other Alternatives

Sometimes the analysis will lead to the conclusion that an option will not work or will make things worse. Advocates should explore all possible alternative options and resources with the woman, including the woman's resources, the advocate's resources, and other agencies' or systems' resources.

Analyzing Legal Options with Jane

Jane told the advocate that she called the police last night because her partner John was scarier than usual. She just wanted someone to take John away until he could sober up and calm down. She wished John could get some help for his drinking. Jane doesn't want John to get in trouble, because if he loses his job she'll have no way to pay the rent or support herself or their new baby.

Describe what choices or decisions Jane can make. Jane lives in a state where there is mandatory arrest for domestic violence crimes. Once Jane calls the police, she will not be able to choose whether or not John is arrested. Jane called the police and they arrested John. In the court where John's case is being handled, the prosecutor makes the decision to prosecute. Jane will not be able to influence that decision. If John is prosecuted and convicted, however, the prosecutor and the judge will listen to what sentence Jane thinks John should receive, including the fact that she wants to stay with John, keep him from going to jail, and get him to go to alcohol counseling. Ultimately, the judge will decide.

Explore the consequences for Jane if she pursues or decides not to pursue a legal option. Because the prosecutor will make the decision whether or not to prosecute John—no matter what Jane thinks—the advocate would focus on the consequences of John's sentence if he is convicted. The prosecutor is not sympathetic to Jane's decision to stay with John, and this might affect how Jane will be treated by this prosecutor in any future domestic violence cases against John. Another consideration is John's reaction to Jane's statement about his drinking and her request that he be ordered to go to alcohol counseling.

Explore other alternatives for Jane. Jane has decided to stay with John. Jane can get support and information from the local domestic violence project. Jane has a large family who cares about her and she can also seek support from them. She has thought about asking her brother to live with them for a while, because she believes John will not hurt her if her brother is there. In addition, Jane could go to Al-Anon. Jane has also decided to talk to John's brother, George, who is a father figure to John, about John's drinking. George has been attending AA meetings for years, and Jane thinks he might be able to get John to realize he needs help with his drinking.

Develop and Implement the Refined Safety Plan

Safety plans are strategies and responses that address the batterer-generated risks identified and prioritized by each battered woman. As discussed in Chapter 5, "Battered Women's Decision Making and Safety Plans," safety plans may include strategies for staying and strategies for leaving, with protection strategies as aspects of each. It is important to keep in mind that women have already been planning and responding to the risks and violence they and their children have faced. Woman-defined advocacy builds on women's plans and avoids preconceived notions of what will make a particular battered woman or her children safe. Collaborative safety plans may be short term or long range, depending on the advocate's role and the time he or she has available. For example, if the advocate's role is to contact women immediately after their partner has been arrested, the collaborative safety plan that results from that contact may be very short-term, perhaps only until the next day, when the woman comes to court. On the other hand, an advocate may be in contact over several years with a particular battered woman who calls the hotline from time to time. This collaborative plan would be ongoing and long range. Safety plans are also ever changing, as battered women respond to their partner's behavior, assess a current strategy, get new or different information, and experience the reaction of outside systems such as the police, social services, courts, and medical and child protective services. Some strategies will make things better for some women and not others, whereas other approaches might work for a while and then be ineffective. Safety planning is an ongoing process.

Identify What Type of Safety Strategies to Pursue

Strategies may include staying or leaving. Strategies may have short-term or long-range time frames. The strategy identified should be based on battered women's decisions.

Identify the Actions Necessary to Implement
the Plan and Clarify Them With the Woman

It is particularly important to clarify with the battered woman what actions she needs to take and what actions the advocate will take. For example, a safety plan for leaving might start with a protective order and divide implementation responsibilities as follows: The advocate goes with the woman to court to get the temporary order. The advocate takes the papers to a sheriff to have them served on the woman's partner. The woman gets certified official copies of the order and gives a copy to her child care provider and the school.

If the actions necessary to implement a safety plan are not taken, the plan will fail. Therefore, it is essential that advocates confirm with each battered woman who will do what before they end the safety planning discussion. Repeat the plan and the expectations. If there are potential life-threatening risks or serious risks to the children, then implementing the plan may involve enhanced advocacy: more time, more activity, more advocacy.

Provide Information About Strategies That May Enhance a
Woman's Safety but Are Not the Focus of Her Current Plan

For example, a battered woman's plan is to stay in the relationship until she can find a full-time job. She told her partner if he hits her again, she will leave immediately. The woman tells the advocate she is sure that her partner will not hit her again now that she has given him the ultimatum. The advocate might say, "I understand you believe it won't happen again—and let's hope it doesn't —but would you like to talk about some things you can do to protect yourself in case it does?"

Tell Her Who She Can Contact if She Needs Help

Safety planning is an ongoing process, and interactions between advocates and battered women are often limited by time and other constraints. Therefore, woman-defined advocacy should anticipate multiple contacts between battered women and advocates. Battered women should leave every interaction with an advocate with information about how to contact the advocate or someone else who will help. A battered woman must know who to contact and what to do if her analysis or plans change or she needs additional information or a clarification.

Enhanced Advocacy

There are times when advocates will want or need to provide enhanced advocacy. Two of these times are when the potential for life-threatening violence exists or when the children are abused or neglected. Enhanced advocacy is not a different kind of advocacy; it simply acknowledges that there are circumstances in which advocates must "do more." Doing more can take many different forms, and, as with all advocacy, will be unique to each battered woman. Enhanced advocacy might include any combination of the following:

- Taking more time with the battered woman
- Having more frequent contact with her, if it is safe to do so
- Making follow-up phone calls or contacts, if it is safe to do so
- Developing and immediately implementing protection strategies
- Expediting processes to get resources or responses for the woman
- Making contacts for referrals directly to ensure a strong, quick connection to another agency's help
- Developing safety plans with children

In all life-threatening or severe violence situations, advocates should include physical violence in the review and develop protection strategies for the woman that include her children. Enhanced advocacy when there are serious risks to the children should include an assessment of whether the advocate should or must, as required by law, make a report or take other unilateral action to protect the children.

In life-threatening situations, advocates may be very afraid for the woman and her children. It is very difficult for an advocate when the advocate believes that a woman with whom he or she is working could be killed. Yet this fear can also lead an advocate to replace a battered woman's decision making with his or her own or to slip into service-defined advocacy. It can be hard not to "take over" when there is extreme danger and manipulate women into pursuing the option that the advocate believes offers the best alternative. For example, the woman's only option is to leave the area and go into hiding. Although this is often the most protective option available to a woman, there are many reasons why a woman might not choose it. If the advocate presents this option first or as the only option, then the woman may not view the advocate as a helpful resource. Therefore, it is important that enhanced advocacy in life-threatening situations, like all other advocacy, start from the woman's perspective and explore her view of risks and options first; then the advocate can present concerns and ideas. Safety plans developed for life-threatening risks must include options chosen by the woman after the advocate provides her with information about options and analyzes them with her.

Barriers to the Creation of Woman-Defined Safety Plans

Advocacy Context

Setting

Advocacy for battered women takes place in many settings, each with particular resources and limitations on the advocate's role. Advocates who work in local domestic violence projects are likely to focus solely on battered women and their children. Although there may be some limitations placed on their work, such as funding requirements, these advocates are fairly free to provide advocacy that is expansive, comprehensive, and responds directly to the woman's analysis and plans.

Different contexts do not always limit advocacy. Whatever the setting, a woman-defined approach will mean the advocate gives and receives better information. Persons providing advocacy who have specialized training, skills, and experience in a particular area may be particularly helpful to battered women in analyzing strategies within that area. For example, a family law attorney who has experience and skill in working with battered women will be able to provide a very accurate analysis of family law strategies such as divorce, custody, child support, and visitation.

Advocacy in other settings may lead to a more limited response to battered women. Whether people providing advocacy can respond directly to battered women's analyses and plans will be determined, in part, by their particular role and legal, practice, or ethical requirements. Some contexts make it more likely that a person providing advocacy will take action that diverges from or is counter to the woman's decisions or plans. For persons whose primary role is advocacy for battered women, this usually arises only when they must report abuse or neglect of a battered woman's children. Yet even these advocates may work within other systems that place additional requirements on them. For example, advocates working for prosecutors must disclose exculpatory evidence—information that could help the defendant in a criminal case. Whatever the context, persons providing advocacy will have requirements and rules that will limit their role. Some of these will be self-imposed, and others will be required by funders, the law, or the system in which they are working. Here are some examples of such limitations:

- The police officer who is required to make an arrest after finding probable cause that a crime was committed
- The health provider who is required by protocol to refer a battered woman to the social work or psychiatric unit
- The prosecutor who is compelled to agree to a lesser charge because of caseload demands or other considerations
- The child protective services worker who is required by protocol to remove a battered woman's children from their home
- The battered woman's advocate working in a domestic violence shelter who cannot offer shelter to a substance-abusing woman because of shelter policy
- The therapist who is required to disclose records or other information about the children to both parents, including the abusive parent

Taking action counter to a battered woman's decisions and plans does not mean a woman-defined approach is abandoned.

Considerations When the Context of Advocacy Raises Limitations

If the advocate's time is limited. As a beginning consideration, if the advocate cannot have more than a cursory discussion with the battered woman because of time or other constraints, then it is essential to refer her to someone who can.

If the advocate cannot further a battered woman's plans or will take action counter to them, refer her to someone who can help. For example, a battered woman may call the police because she wants her abusive partner to be arrested and removed from the home. A police officer may not make an arrest because the officer has determined she does not have the legal authority to make the arrest. The police officer should identify other resources, such as a local domestic violence project, that can help the woman pursue other strategies for getting her partner out of the home.

If the advocate cannot further a battered woman's plans or will take action counter to them, the advocate should explain what he or she is doing and why. When an advocate takes action counter to a woman's decisions or plans, the advocate should tell the woman what action he or she is taking and explain why he or she is taking it. This explanation may help the woman's future planning. For example, a judge might explain, "I'm not ordering your husband out of the home, because I don't have proof that he actually knows about this court date." If there are aspects of the action over which the woman does have some choice, the advocate should explore these with her. For example, a police officer may tell the woman he cannot make an arrest because he does not have probable cause. The officer may then ask the woman if she would like to file a statement for the record or if she would like him to take her to the domestic violence shelter or other safe location.

If the advocate cannot further a battered woman's plans or will take action counter to them, the advocate should give the battered woman information about alternatives and her rights. For example, a court officer may recommend that the court enter a protective order that removes a woman's partner from the home—even though the woman wants the partner to remain in the home. The court officer should tell the woman that she has the right to speak to the prosecutor or judge directly to tell them her wishes.

It is also important to explore if there are any actions that would minimize the harm. For example, a battered woman may tell the prosecutor, "If my husband thinks I'm cooperating with you to get him out of the house, he'll kill me." The prosecutor may then offer to subpoena the woman and make it clear in court that he is forcing her to do this. The prosecutor should be honest with the woman when this strategy might not work. For example, a particular judge might always ask the woman, in front of the defendant, whether or not she wants him out of the house, or her partner's attorney might have the opportunity to ask such questions.

Service-Defined Advocacy

A challenge to woman-defined advocacy arises when advocacy focuses exclusively on getting women to use resources, options, or services. These services and resources may include

- A hotline
- Individual, family, or couples' counseling
- Child advocacy
- Parenting education

- Support
- Support groups
- Shelter
- Legal advocacy
- Legal remedies: restraining orders, police, arrest, divorce, custody, child support
- Referrals to other services
- Housing advocacy

When providing these services is the only goal, whether or not they fit into a battered woman's risk analysis or safety plans, the advocate is using *service-defined advocacy*. Conversely, with woman-defined advocacy, the services provided fit into the battered woman's risk analysis and plans. In other words, service-defined advocacy tries to fit the woman into the service, and woman-defined advocacy fits the service into the woman's plans. It is important to clarify from the outset that providing services is part of the essential work of all domestic violence advocates. Providing services should be distinguished from advocacy that is defined by services, however.

Lana, a Court-Based Advocate

Lana is a court-based battered woman's advocate. Cathy's husband was arrested last night for beating her up. Lana calls Cathy and spends the entire conversation explaining to Cathy what a protective order is and what Cathy should do to enforce it. Cathy tells Lana she doesn't want one and asks for information about helping her husband get out of jail. Lana tells Cathy she should worry about herself, not her husband, and continues to talk about why Cathy should ask for a protective order.

Lana is providing service-defined advocacy because the exclusive focus of her advocacy is providing Cathy with a protective order. Lana has not asked Cathy why she does not want a protective order, whether a protective order would enhance her safety, why she wants her husband out of jail, or about her current safety plans. Clearly, Lana is trying to force Cathy to use a protective order (fit her to the service) rather than exploring if the protective order fits Cathy's safety strategies.

Providing information about a protective order may be a part of woman-defined advocacy as well. Simply providing information about protective orders, however, no matter what the battered woman is saying, is defining advocacy by the service. It is the latter, service-defined advocacy, that has serious implications for battered women and their children.

Service-defined advocacy may come from the best intentions—to help battered women use the services available. Yet, if advocacy focuses on the risks addressed by the service and not necessarily the risks perceived by the woman to be her priority, unintended and negative consequences can follow. For example, an advocate may begin to label or blame a woman for failing to use the service, or focus her energies and resources on women who are "ready" to accept what the advocate has to offer. Loseke (1992) found that this kind of process was used implicitly by staff in the shelter she studied. She writes,

> The practice of client selection was . . . practical activity oriented to maintaining an acceptable number of clients and to selecting appropriate clients. . . . An "appropriate client" was a woman who workers felt *could be* and *should be* served given current "space availability.". . . [The criteria were] if she was judged to *need emergency housing* . . . [if she wanted] *the full range of . . . services* . . . [if she] wanted services for a *particular reason* . . . [especially if she wanted] to be helped out of the situation . . . [or] really wanted to make changes . . . *because she was a battered woman* . . . [and was] deemed capable of living communally. (pp. 74-78)

In addition, trying to fit women's lives and realities into available options is less efficient. Advocates may waste time talking to women about options that are irrelevant to their circumstances and lead some women to believe the advocate does not understand their situation, thereby destroying the chance to establish a collaborative, trusting relationship. Ultimately, service-defined advocacy can lead to ineffective safety planning.

Another limitation of service-defined advocacy is that most of the services are designed for battered women who are about to leave their relationships. For example, shelter, restraining orders, divorces, child support, and housing advocacy all assume that the woman will separate from her partner right away. Most of the services listed in the left column of Figure 7.1 (at the end of the chapter) could be described as external interventions designed to help a woman get out of her relationship or survive once she has left. The few services that do exist for women staying in their relationships, such as counseling and support groups, often have a goal of helping women get ready to leave. Services geared toward leaving will not respond to the many battered women whose safety plans involve remaining in their relationship.

Service-defined advocacy may not enhance a woman's safety and may even increase her risks. When advocates do not start with battered women's analyses and plans, they will not be able to assess if a particular service can help or make things worse.

Wanda

Wanda called the hotline because her alcoholic husband started drinking again after 8 months of being dry. When he's drinking, she's afraid he might get violent. Rita, the hotline counselor, suggests Wanda get a restraining order to kick her husband out of the house.

Rita does not check out Wanda's risk analysis or safety plans. Therefore, she recommends an order to Wanda without knowing that

- Wanda does not want to end her marriage,
- Wanda relies on her husband's income, and
- Wanda filed for a restraining order one other time and her husband went on a drinking binge for 4 weeks, often driving by the house at all hours of the day and night. He told her if she "ever tried that again he'd kill her and the kids."

Without analyzing the implications of a service for each particular woman, the advocate may increase the woman's risks.

Resource limitations also contribute to a significant number of requirements, conditions, and barriers among the systems that respond to battered women. Among the more obvious barriers are language, cost, and the hours the particular resource is available, such as "normal business hours." In addition, most social services have income, geographic, and other conditions. For example, in one agency a woman must be poor, live in the area where the service is located, and be battered. At the same time she must not have other issues such as substance abuse, mental disability, or AIDS. In another agency, only women with substance abuse, a mental disability, or AIDS would be eligible for help. As nonprofit and social service funding continues to shrink, agencies are likely to increase conditions as they set priorities to serve the "neediest" or most "treatable" in the community.

Sometimes a strategy to prioritize and limit the work leads to service-defined advocacy. Most advocates responding to domestic violence have limited resources, and few can offer truly comprehensive responses. Therefore, service specialization becomes the basis for limit setting. For example, a shelter worker provides shelter and support, the lawyer provides representation in civil cases, the court-based advocate provides information in criminal court on the day of arraignment, and the doctor provides medical care. Although this makes sense in terms of professional training and limitations, it also significantly limits the assistance a battered woman receives from any one source. Advocates that provide particular services can begin to focus exclusively on providing those services, without regard for a battered woman's perspective or other options available to her. Building comprehensive services and more effective collaborative relationships among service providers is discussed in Part III.

Implications of Service-Defined Advocacy and Barriers to Understanding

Service-defined advocacy can create a gap between battered women and advocates, with the advocate on one side and the battered woman on the other. When advocacy is limited to getting women to use a particular service, then women's strategies and power may be undervalued or even dismissed completely. The realities of the woman's life might be ignored. Resources that the woman is already relying on or planning to use—such as her family, a religious institution, friends, or employer—may be ignored in the service-defined safety plan, leaving the battered woman with an incomplete safety strategy. In addition, many of the barriers that have always kept women and advocates separated, such as race, class, culture, and life experience, continue to do so in a service-defined advocacy approach. To the extent that services are often created by the dominant culture, service-defined advocacy may even exacerbate these differences.

Figure 7.1 was developed to illustrate the various challenges to woman-defined advocacy. It shows a number of factors that can cause a gap between the advocate and the battered woman. These factors might include the assumption that leaving is the exclusive safety strategy for all battered women, or that fitting women into the services

Advocate's Resources	Barriers That Keep Advocates on Their Side of the Gap*	Woman's Resources

Examples:
 	
Hotline
Counseling
Child advocacy
Parenting support
Legal advocacy
Support groups
Shelter
Legal remedies, i.e.,
  restraining orders
  arrest
  divorce, custody
  child support
Referrals
Housing advocacy
	Service-defined advocacy
	Physical violence as the priority
	Leaving as the primary strategy
	
	*Other issues that can keep advocates
	from collaborating with women:*
	  Communication
	  Class
	  Race
	  Culture
	  Life experience
	  Education
	  Language
	  Fear
	  Priorities
	  Time pressures
	  Perceptions
	  System she works in
	  Funding/Funders
	  Religion
	  Attitude
		Examples:
		
		Knowledge
		Skills
		Experience
		Training
		Family
		Children
		Home
		Job
		Religion
		Partner
		Friends
		Neighbors
		Money
		Others

Figure 7.1. Challenges to Woman-Defined Advocacy

SOURCE: © Greater Hartford Legal Assistance, Inc. Used with permission.

*There are also barriers to women crossing the gap, including their partners, their perceptions, the fact that it may not be worth crossing because advocates cannot provide what women want or need. Sometimes what advocates have available on their side of the gap has very little relevance or use to women seeking to end violence in their relationship. The focus here is on the advocate's role.

available is the sole goal of advocacy. Additional factors are the barriers to advocates' understanding women's perspectives.

PART III

SYSTEMS ADVOCACY

One of the premises of woman-defined advocacy for individual battered women is that advocates must work with the realities and options available to each woman. This approach to advocacy clearly identifies the limitations of battered women's options, including the limitations of systems responding to them. Advocacy that helps guide battered women through systems that offer few, poor, or no options is pragmatic and, one hopes, helpful, but ultimately only makes the best of a less-than-ideal situation. If a system does not respond or responds poorly, then battered women have fewer options for their safety and the safety of their children. Therefore, a natural part of advocacy for individual battered women is advocacy to enhance systemic responses to battered women. The more and better options available, the more likely battered women and their children will be safe. Policy advocacy in the legal, health, government, mental health, child protection, and social service systems is an integral part of woman-defined advocacy.

Justice for battered women cannot be achieved if advocacy is solely helping women maneuver through systems that may be ineffective or unresponsive. Advocates do the best they can to help battered women with what is available, but must also identify what battered women need. This is not easy. One place to begin is within the advocate's own agency. Chapter 8, "Toward a Woman-Defined Advocacy Environment," discusses how advocates can work to make their own agency woman defined. Yet we cannot stop there. All systems that respond to battered women need the attention, insight, and analysis of battered women and their advocates. A woman-defined approach to policy advocacy is presented in Chapter 9, "Woman-Defined Policy Advocacy."[1]

Note

1. Although the term "women-defined" would be technically more accurate for policy advocacy that responds to the needs of many women, this book uses the term "woman-defined" advocacy for ease of use and to emphasize the inclusion of policy advocacy in the overall model.

8

Toward a Woman-Defined
Advocacy Environment

The environment in which an advocate works can have a significant effect on her advocacy. An agency (the word *agency* is used to describe any place in which there is advocacy for battered women) may provide a supportive workplace, where all staff work together to back battered women's efforts to be safe, thereby strengthening each advocate's ability to help. An agency may have policies and practices that perpetuate service-defined advocacy. Another agency may "talk the talk" of empowerment and advocacy built on women's decision making, but not "walk the walk" for some or all of the women with whom it works. These types of agencies would limit an advocate's options. A woman-defined advocacy agency provides the opportunity for individual woman-defined advocacy to occur and does its own business in a way that is woman defined. Building and sustaining an environment in which advocates effectively use their knowledge and resources and the battered women define the advocacy can be difficult. Organizational change is a broad and complex topic; therefore, this chapter can present only key elements for creating a woman-defined advocacy environment, the challenges of making such changes, and some thoughts on how to begin.

For woman-defined advocacy to flourish, advocates need an environment that provides certain basic elements: The agency must demonstrate its commitment to providing woman-defined advocacy; the role of the advocate must be defined broadly, and advocates must be given the freedom and support to respond to the uniqueness and complexity of battered women; and the agency must actively pursue strong collaborative working relationships with other agencies.

Agency Commitment to
Provide Woman-Defined Advocacy

An agency's commitment is demonstrated by what it says ("the talk") and what it does ("the walk"). There is no clearer demonstration of an agency's commitment than the day-to-day provision of advocacy. The environment of the agency and the advocacy it provides is built each day in every aspect of the agency's functions. All the work of the agency is relevant, from the way the first contact with a battered woman is handled to the discussion of shelter rules at a staff meeting to a policy position the agency will take. To institutionalize this commitment, to make it part of and supported by every aspect of the agency, requires ongoing, vigilant analysis and effort.

Although most agencies that primarily provide advocacy to battered women, such as domestic violence shelters, would readily state that they believe battered women should control their own decision making and lives, this may not be how the agency is viewed by battered women, the agency's staff, or the public. Therefore, an agency seeking to demonstrate its commitment needs to consider the messages it conveys to battered women and others about the work it does and how it does it.

An agency may use a variety of methods to describe its work. One method is the formal organizational documents of the agency. These might include a mission statement formally adopted by the agency's governing body, bylaws, or other legal documents that establish the agency's legal status. Mission statements and the governing structure of the agency can set the parameters for all the agency's work. For example, an agency's bylaws might require that a certain percentage of the board of directors positions be filled by current or formerly battered women to ensure that the agency's oversight and direction includes the perspective of some battered women. This alone will not fully reflect battered women's diverse perspectives, so an agency may also include in its principles a commitment to seek the opinion, perspective, and experience of a variety of battered women regularly, including those the agency does not regularly serve.

The agency's principles will also be reflected in other documents, such as personnel and procedure manuals. For example, the commitment to woman-defined advocacy might be listed as a job qualification, and procedures for covering a hotline or responding to a request for advocacy could outline the approach. Forms tend to guide an advocate's response to women, and therefore careful attention should be paid to the effect agency forms have on advocacy. Forms designed solely to gather information the agency "needs," rather than allowing the advocate to gather information the woman needs the advocate to understand, will limit advocacy. Fund-raising and priority-setting initiatives also establish the direction and nature of the agency's work and reflect its approach to advocacy.

For many agencies responding to family violence, public education and community outreach are integral parts of the work. These efforts may include development and distribution of pamphlets, appearances on radio and television, public speaking, and training. Each of these forums provides different opportunities to talk about domestic violence, battered women, and the agency's work. The information conveyed about battered women, in particular, will reflect the agency's approach to advocacy. For example, a presentation about advocacy that does not acknowledge the ongoing safety planning of battered women reflects an approach that is more advocate defined than one built on a working partnership with battered women. Such a presentation also provides a description of battered women that diminishes their strength and resourcefulness in responding to their partner's violence. Careful consideration of the messages delivered in public presentations is an important beginning to a commitment to woman-defined advocacy. Yet, statements alone do not create such an environment for advocates or the reality of such advocacy for the battered women with whom they work.

Demonstrating and providing a woman-defined advocacy environment is not easy. Agency self-analysis that starts collaboratively can easily deteriorate into finger pointing and counterproductive conflict. Skilled leadership is required to avoid such a negative result. Whether part of a traditional hierarchy or an aspect of a more shared model, there is no substitute for the guidance of skilled leadership. Leadership can provide the planning, process, and implementation necessary to move forward constructively. Therefore, a commitment to provide woman-defined advocacy will include a commitment to build the leadership necessary to realize such a goal. Such leaders will have a thorough understanding of woman-defined advocacy and its application, as well as the skills to teach and guide its use by other staff and the agency as a whole.

Role and Support of Advocates

Advocates are the heart of a woman-defined advocacy environment. Therefore, the strength and welfare of the advocates will determine the overall nature of the agency's advocacy. For advocates to flourish, they need clearly established parameters and expectations for their advocacy, the resources necessary to meet those expectations, and a broad range of support. Multiple and conflicting goals will cause confusion for advocates and battered women and may result in unnecessary conflict with the systems in which the advocate works. Clearly established and communicated expectations will enhance advocates' work with battered women and help reduce the stress of that work.

The parameters and expectations of advocacy will establish the approach, tasks, or "job description" for advocacy, determine what training and skills are necessary, and facilitate collaboration with others responding to family violence. Advocacy for battered women is difficult and complex, pulling advocates in a variety of directions. As discussed in Chapter 5, "Battered Women's Decision Making and Safety Plans," the goal of advocacy is determined by a variety of factors. These factors include the context of the advocacy, such as a court, domestic violence shelter, or health care system; conditions set by a funding source; legal requirements; and the guidelines of the advocate's agency. The factors may lead to a common understanding of the goals or to conflicting views. The conflict can create additional pressure and demands on advocates.

Service-defined advocacy can reflect and reinforce different goals. For example, a child protection worker's service-defined approach is to require battered mothers always to go to a shelter. A service-defined domestic violence project advocate always works with battered mothers to obtain protective orders that would remove abusive partners from the home and allow the mothers to remain in the home. These two service-defined approaches are in direct conflict with each other and may also conflict with battered mothers' safety plans.

No matter what factors influence advocacy goals, most advocates have victim safety and offender accountability as the ultimate goals of their work. Although there may be agreement on these larger goals, advocacy gets more difficult when there are different objectives for meeting these goals. For example, court staff may believe the goals will be met through prosecution and conviction of offenders. An advocate may believe the goals can be met through prosecution and conviction only if they do not increase the batterer-generated or life-generated risks women face. In a circumstance in which prosecution will increase a woman's risks, the advocate may have a different view of his or her role than the prosecutor. The advocate may try to find ways to facilitate the prosecution and help the woman stay safe. If this is not possible, however, the advocate may see his or her role as reducing risks by discouraging the prosecution. This could cause conflict with court staff unless there is a shared view of the advocate's role.

Generally, a broad view of advocacy will expand an advocate's opportunity to build on battered women's current safety plans. The narrower the response, the more likely the advocacy will be service defined. What woman-defined advocates do—help battered women by integrating their knowledge and resources into the woman's analysis and plans—requires flexibility. Flexibility allows advocates to build on women's current plans and respond to the complex and diverse needs of battered women. For example, an advocate's role may be to help battered women find housing. An advocate with flexibility might help the woman with any of the following:

- Go to a domestic violence shelter for a few days, a year, or more.
- Find a real estate agent, friendly landlord, or subsidized housing program.
- Refer her to a community housing agency or make the call himself or herself.
- Go with the woman to look at available housing and support her as she signs the lease or contract to buy.
- Find child care while the woman searches for housing.
- Get priority status on housing waiting lists.
- Get a court order to remove her abusive partner from their current home.
- Get money to help pay the security deposit.
- Get a mortgage.

This example also illustrates how service-defined advocacy can limit an advocate's options to help battered women. If an advocate's response is limited to providing domestic violence shelter services, then the advocate limits her ability to help the battered woman find housing.

It may be difficult for an agency to provide an advocate with such freedom and resources. The agency would need the funding to support a broad range of activities, which might require an explanation of the need for such an advocate role to funders, and others may need to be convinced that such advocate flexibility is crucial. Also, the agency would need to provide support and supervision to advocates working in diverse environments. Collaboration with other agencies and disciplines is another way to obtain access to the range of resources advocates will need.

Individual woman-defined advocacy brings advocates into the diverse analyses and plans of battered women. This could mean discussing substance abuse with one woman and immigration issues with another. Because expertise in all areas is not possible, what skills and knowledge should advocates have? An agency should try to ensure that its advocates know enough about fundamental areas to identify the issues the woman is talking about, when the woman needs to have additional help, who could provide the help, and how the woman can access that resource. Advocates also need to have a good sense of what they do not know and when they need to say to women, "I don't know, I'm not the right person to help you with that, but I'll work with you to find someone who can." For example, an advocate may work with a battered woman who defended herself when her partner attacked her. He was seriously injured. The advocate should know the woman could be arrested and charged with a crime and therefore needs a criminal defense lawyer's advice, along with the advocate's continued support and advocacy in other areas.

Woman-defined advocacy requires advocates to walk a fine line, respectfully helping a woman get where she thinks she should go on one side, and leading a woman where the advocate thinks she should go on the other. It can be very difficult to discern the difference between giving women information about certain risks and options with the *result* of leading them in a certain direction and giving them certain information with the *goal* of leading them in the direction the advocate wants them to go. An agency can help its advocates know when they have "crossed the line" by providing them with ongoing constructive and supportive opportunities to think, talk, and learn about their advocacy. For example, with ongoing analysis, an advocate may discover that she tends to take over decision making for certain types of women or women facing certain types of risks. This awareness places the advocate in a better position to avoid taking over in such situations in the future. There are situations when an advocate may have to cross the line, such as when there is the risk of lethal violence, risk of suicide, or the abuse or neglect of children. These are particularly stressful and difficult situations for advocates and call for advanced preparation, access to immediate guidance and direction, along with follow-up debriefing and assessment. The uniqueness of women's needs requires advocates to learn from the experience of each interaction with a battered woman.

In addition to skills and knowledge, advocates need support. Advocates listen and develop a custom response for each battered woman, know that some women will be hit again and a few may even be killed, feel the frustration when women have few options, and know there is little that will be done to "change" the batterer. These are difficult realities to face; eventually, they can take their toll. Advocates could become less effective and engaged in their work. They might lean toward service-defined advocacy, with its clear limits on role and responsibility and its appearance of providing a solution. This is understandable and predictable, particularly if the agency is under-staffed and under-resourced.

An agency can provide both systemic and personal support to advocates. Advocates should feel the agency is behind them. At times, advocates must put pressure on systems or persons responding to family violence. The agency must do advance work to prepare systems for such advocacy, but must also be there for individual advocates when conflict arises. Personal support for advocates can take a variety of forms, such as simply acknowledging the stress, giving advocates the opportunity to vent and talk about their experiences, assigning a variety of advocacy tasks to offer some respite, making work schedules as flexible as possible, providing quality supervision, and encouraging regular use of vacation time. These actions should be integrated into the agency's policies and procedures.

To provide woman-defined advocacy to every woman every time, advocates need a supportive and constructive environment. Staff must understand and respect the work each person does and have a shared view of the work. This does not mean staff have to be "one big happy family," ending each day with a group hug, or that everyone thinks the same way or would approach a particular advocacy situation in an identical manner. In fact, the environment needs to be built with a staff with diverse backgrounds, experiences, and racial or ethnic identities. A diverse staff will strengthen the agency's ability to help battered women only if that staff has a meaningful opportunity to influence the work of the agency as a whole.

Collaborative Working Relationships

Collaborative working relationships support both the individual and systemic advocacy of an agency. On a practical individual advocacy level, the amount and diversity of advocacy needed to implement battered women's safety plans cannot be provided by any one agency. Advocacy that is part of a larger collaborative environment will provide battered women with quicker, more comprehensive, and relevant responses. In addition, advocates who are familiar with other responding agencies because of ongoing joint efforts will be better informed about the options available and will be better able to assist women in their analysis of those options.

Policy advocacy, discussed in Chapter 9, "Woman-Defined Policy Advocacy," requires that agencies collaborate to assess current responses and work together to improve them. Collaborative relationships formed to help individual battered women can be the basis for this broader work. An agency's commitment to woman-defined advocacy will take advocacy beyond work with individual battered women to join with others to address the range of issues affecting battered women and children. This will come in part from collaboration and in part from an understanding that both batterer-generated and life-generated risks keep battered women from being safe.

Sometimes collaboration is done through a formal, preestablished protocol, and at other times it is done informally by simply picking up the phone to talk with a person at another agency. Whatever the form, communication is the key to successful collaboration. Although a key aspect to collaboration is sharing information, agencies must be cautious about disclosing information about individual battered women. Battered women will be more likely to share information with advocates if they know it will remain confidential. Because individual woman-defined advocacy relies on accurate and thorough information gathering, agencies must protect battered women's privacy.

Changing the Advocacy Environment

Elements of Woman-Defined Advocacy

Provide systemic woman-defined advocacy.

- Build a woman-defined advocacy environment.
  - Choose an approach.
  - Establish the elements of a woman-defined advocacy environment.

▲ Demonstrate a commitment to provide woman-defined advocacy.

▲ Define the role of the advocate broadly enough, and give advocates the freedom, time, resources, and support to respond to the uniqueness and complexity of battered women, while maintaining battered women's privacy.

▲ Pursue strong collaborative working relationships with other agencies.

Choose an Approach

There are numerous approaches to organizational change, many of which include complex systems, planning, and leadership styles. This section suggests two ways to get started: one reactive and informal, the other proactive and formal. Both approaches begin with making a commitment to providing individual woman-defined advocacy.

Like individual woman-defined advocacy, the approach to changing an agency is an ongoing process that must acknowledge success, admit limitations, and respectfully work toward a better future. Overall, changing the advocacy environment is more likely to be successful if one tries to build new and more effective approaches rather than seek to place blame for real or perceived failures of current advocacy. A positive approach that validates current stresses and challenges for advocates will encourage the self-analysis, change, and risk taking necessary to shift the direction of the organization's work.

Reactive Approach: Provide Individual
Woman-Defined Advocacy and Then
Respond as Agency Issues Arise

If even the thought of taking on something new is overwhelming, then be reassured that this work can and should be done as part of the ongoing work of the agency. Most agencies already have processes for long- and short-term planning, developing job descriptions, and providing orientation, training, and supervision to staff. Agencies are typically already part of collaborative relationships with other agencies. Each agency will have strengths on which to build, and some will find there are few changes to make. If you think your agency has a lot of work to do, try not to let the scope of the work keep you from making any progress. No agency is a perfect place for advocacy. Just get started. The process of strengthening or shifting to woman-defined advocacy can begin simply by asking yourself, "What do we do for battered women?" "How do we do it?" and "Does it help?"

A reactive approach does not mean there is no planning or forethought about the process. On the contrary, this ongoing agency self-analysis must be deliberately institutionalized into the way the agency does its business. See Appendix A, "Considerations for Information Gathering," for information about documenting the work of an agency. This includes ensuring that the opportunity, resources, and leadership are in place to react to and address issues that arise.

As advocates provide individual woman-defined advocacy and participate in the ongoing discussions needed to implement it, new and different issues will arise. It may become clear that the agency needs to develop different resources and options. Some agency rules and procedures may become irrelevant to or counter individual advocacy goals.

Helen

Helen's safety plan is to remain in her relationship indefinitely. She believes she'll be all right if she can find some ongoing support and a sense that someone cares about her. Cindy, an advocate working with Helen to enhance her staying strategy, tries to identify ongoing sources of such support. They consider family, friends, Helen's clergy person, and Cindy's agency. Unfortunately, the only support groups offered by the agency are time limited and focus on supporting women as they leave relationships. Cindy understands that these groups will not meet Helen's needs. She identifies the need for her agency to develop and provide an ongoing support group for battered women who are staying.

Proactive Approach: Provide Individual
Woman-Defined Advocacy, Analyze Current
Practice, and Implement Necessary Changes

A proactive approach would begin with an analysis of current advocacy. Once the information gathering and analysis are complete, the agency must determine what change, if any, is necessary; plan how to make necessary change; and implement that plan. The analysis could be of the entire agency or of a particular aspect, such as the intake system. Issues to consider in that analysis are almost limitless. Here are some suggestions:

- What are battered women's perceptions of the agency and its advocacy?
- How does the agency's advocacy affect battered women's safety plans?
- What do paid and current volunteer advocates think about the agency's work, its policies, and procedures? What would they change to further their advocacy?
- Do current forms, guidelines, eligibility requirements, and intake procedures foster partnerships with battered women?
- How do funders influence advocacy?
- Does the agency raise funds to support woman-defined advocacy needs, such as transportation and child care?
- Does the agency provide an environment where woman-defined advocacy can flourish?
  - Is there a genuine commitment by the agency for battered women to have control over their lives?
  - Is the role of advocacy defined broadly enough, and are advocates given the freedom and support necessary to fulfill that role?
  - Does the agency have strong collaborative working relationships with other agencies and maintain battered women's privacy?

(Appendix A, "Considerations for Information Gathering," provides additional guidance on information gathering and analysis.)

Domestic Violence Project

A local domestic violence project's policy is to allow each battered woman a 2-month stay at the shelter and to prohibit contact with her partner while she is there. The bases for the policy are the assumption that women come to the shelter as part of a plan to leave their relationships permanently; allowing more than one stay will keep women from making the most of their time in the shelter; women need the full 2 months to get their lives in order; and there is limited shelter space. In addition, project staff believe contact with the partner will weaken a woman's resolve to leave and perhaps allow him to find her and hurt her or the shelter staff or residents.

Analysis. This policy assumes that a battered woman who comes to the shelter plans to leave her relationship permanently, and does not allow for or support activities other than immediate plans for leaving. It does not acknowledge the other types of plans a battered woman may have, including long-range plans for leaving or safety plans for staying. For example, a battered woman's plan may be to stay in the relationship, but leave temporarily when her partner is on a drinking binge and, in her experience, is most likely to be violent. Prohibiting contact with a partner also assumes the relationship is over and may preclude a woman from gathering essential safety planning information, such as her partner's mood and activities since she has left, where he is living, what he is doing, and his thoughts on his behavior and her leaving. In addition, the policy does not anticipate that women's plans may change or that 2 months may not be the ideal shelter stay for every battered woman.

Plans to change this particular policy might include an exploration of how the shelter could be used to enhance women's safety plans for staying. For example, allowing women to sign up for a shorter shelter stay may be one possibility that could also address the important issue of limited shelter space. Another possibility is to provide support and advocacy to women staying in the shelter who plan to stay in the relationship. Rethinking the "no contact with partner" rule would also be part of the analysis, including the consideration of how contact with an abusive partner might enhance a woman's overall safety planning.

Demonstrate a Commitment to Provide
Individual Woman-Defined Advocacy

Training or Orientation

Introduction to the concepts of woman-defined advocacy may be included in a number of ways: as part of a formal training program, as part of the ongoing in-service training of a staff, or as part of an orientation program. Whatever the format, the following are key components.

The trainers. Trainers should be skilled in training, well versed in the concepts of woman-defined advocacy, and credible to the audience. Credibility may require that one of the trainers be from the group being trained. For example, a police training should include a trainer who is a police officer. In addition, at least one of the trainers should have direct experience using woman-defined advocacy. A team approach to training can meet all these needs, facilitate collaboration between the trainer's agencies, and model a collaborative approach to advocacy for the participants.

The training process. Some aspects of the training should be experiential. Advocates will need to use aspects of this approach to understand the challenges. It is important to provide advocates with some opportunity to look critically, yet supportively, at their current approach to advocacy so they can begin to see how it may differ from a more woman-defined approach. This opportunity is particularly important for training current advocates. Although new advocates may simply see woman-defined advocacy as the way advocacy is done, current advocates will assess whether woman-defined advocacy is any different from what they do now. If an advocate incorrectly concludes that he or she is currently doing woman-defined advocacy, it can be very difficult to help the advocate change the current approach.

Tone. The training should model the approach. In other words, trainers need to be able to understand the advocate's perspective and current approach to advocacy, then carefully and respectfully review that approach and build a partnership for learning and implementing a new approach. The trainers' tone is very important. This is one reason why a trainer who has gone through a shift in approach and who currently does advocacy is so useful. This trainer can talk about different approaches and reinforce that the goal of the training is not to blame anyone for doing advocacy "wrong," but to discuss a woman-defined approach and how it may help advocates help battered women.

Training only on the woman-defined advocacy approach will not fully prepare a person to advocate with battered women. There are many substantive areas in which advocates must be competent, including crisis intervention, homicide and suicide assessment and intervention, substance abuse basics, effects of domestic violence on children and other children's issues, cultural diversity, legal remedies, community resources and programs, protecting confidentiality and privacy, agency procedures, and any other skills relevant to their particular advocacy role.

Ongoing Efforts to Enhance
Individual Woman-Defined Advocacy

Training alone will not provide advocates with all they need to provide woman-defined advocacy. The skills, analysis, and knowledge needed require practice and ongoing support. This can occur as part of regular supervision or case review. Peer support or supervision is an effective model for enhancing skills. Talking with another staff member is often less threatening, is more timely, and provides a more diverse variety of perspectives than traditional hierarchical supervision. Whatever the format, any discussion of advocacy with a particular woman should include asking and answering the following questions: What does the battered woman say and think about [fill in the blank]? What are the risks she includes in her analysis? What does she want, say she needs, fear, think about her children?

Creating an environment in which it is safe for advocates to look critically at their current approach requires someone to begin that process. If you want others to change, demonstrate that you are willing to change. A way to build capacity for change is to take the time to identify and acknowledge progress. That does not mean failures should be ignored. Failures provide an enormous opportunity to learn. Yet, if the analysis of advocacy focuses solely on failures, it will be difficult for advocates to take the risks they need to increase the breadth and quality of their advocacy.

Building this environment can begin with the commitment to learn how to give supportive, constructive feedback. This is a basic communication skill that can be the foundation for progress. If used consistently and well, constructive feedback can facilitate trust, learning, support, and growth.

Discussion of a particular case or advocacy situation may lead to strong disagreements among advocates. Consider whether advocates who hold different positions are also members of different groups, as when advocates of color are on one side and white advocates are on the other. These disagreements may also fall along ethnic, class, gender, sexual orientation, or job classification lines within the agency. Such alignments are important to notice and discuss. The discussion will provide the opportunity to learn, confront bias, and ultimately provide better advocacy to battered women. Staff diversity will not translate into culturally sensitive advocacy or a woman-defined advocacy environment unless the experiences, observations, and opinions of all staff are consciously and deliberately integrated into the agency's work. The final two steps toward a woman-defined advocacy environment follow.

- Define the role of the advocate broadly enough, and give advocates the freedom and support, to respond to the uniqueness and complexity of battered women.
  - Set clear, but flexible expectations and parameters for advocacy.
  - Provide advocates with the training and information they need to meet those expectations.
  - Provide both systemic and personal support to advocates.
- Pursue strong collaborative working relationships with other agencies.
  - Be informed about the other agency, its work, its constituency, and its mission.
  - Share information about the agency, its work, and its mission. Consider "job swapping" or spending time with workers from other agencies as they do their jobs.
  - Approach other agencies respectfully, with a goal of building a partnership.
  - Look for opportunities to collaborate on specific tasks, projects, or initiatives.
  - Assign staff and resources to build collaboration.
  - Establish protocols that maintain battered women's privacy.

9

Woman-Defined
Policy Advocacy

W oman-defined policy advocacy is a natural extension of the work with individual battered women. The direction of woman-defined policy advocacy is evolving as advocates learn from their experiences using the approach. Like the organizational changes discussed in Chapter 8, "Toward a Woman-Defined Advocacy Environment," policy advocacy is a broad and complex topic. This chapter provides an overview of the evolving assumptions on which a woman-defined policy analysis could be based and a process for that analysis.

In this chapter, the term *policy advocacy* is used to describe a wide spectrum of activity on behalf of battered women. It includes working to change the systems responding to domestic violence, such as the legal, health, social service, and child protection systems (e.g., see Peled, Jaffe, & Edleson, 1995). It also includes efforts to ensure that policies—whether administrative, legislative, or programmatic—are implemented in ways that reflect their intent and are monitored for effectiveness. Policy advocacy might encompass the following kinds of decisions to make on particular issues:

- What information will be included in training and how it will be presented
- How to respond to legislation
- What projects will be developed and how these new initiatives will be implemented

- What funding is pursued for broad initiatives and what funding is made available for which activities
- How priorities will be set for the use of limited resources
- What research should be conducted for what reasons and how it will be conducted
- How systems should respond to family violence

A woman-defined approach to policy advocacy takes place in the context of policy work in general. Policy advocacy is by nature the work of compromise and negotiation. It involves balancing interests and the exercise of power and influence. Which interests are balanced, where the compromises are made, and how power and influence are exercised are both day-to-day and long-term questions for policy advocates. Should the majority of battered women benefit—even if it means a few battered women will be significantly excluded or harmed? How will an advocate know if a particular policy will benefit or harm groups of battered women or particular individuals? How will battered women participate in the policy process? How should the issues of racism and other biases be addressed? What positions will not be compromised? Who should make decisions about policy positions and how should they be made? These will be difficult questions to answer.

Unlike individual advocacy, woman-defined policy advocacy must take broad brush strokes. It is not as easy to "check in" with all battered women as it is to understand an individual woman's perspective. Even if this were possible, listening to many battered women will elicit a variety of perspectives, needs, and concerns. Listening alone will not provide the answer, but will identify the range of interests to be balanced.

Although all battered women have the battering and control of a partner in common, there are many differences among individual battered women. It can be extremely challenging to identify, consider, and address the individual differences of battered women in broad-brush policy advocacy. Practically speaking, it is impossible to address each set of individual circumstances at a policy level. There are two aspects to this challenge: first, identifying the range of differences, a process discussed later in this chapter; and second, deciding which position to take when it will help some women, be unhelpful to others, and perhaps harmful to some. One way to decide which position to take is to determine which position will potentially help the most women—the "majority rules" approach. For example, if a local hospital protocol will potentially help 60% of the women coming into the emergency room get more information about domestic violence, will not be relevant to 30% because they will not be identified by the protocol, and hurt 10%, then the protocol will help the majority and would be supported under this approach.

Another way to make policy decisions is to consider the relative harm or benefit to particular groups of individuals. In the above example, the hospital's protocol would potentially help 60% and definitely harm 10%. Under this approach, further analysis of the extent of the harm would be necessary. If the harm were life-threatening, analysis would be easier and the protocol would not be supported. Ordinarily, the consequences will not be so clear. Most policy analysis requires a certain amount of guessing about what the interests of individual battered women are, how the policy would be implemented, and the potential effect on battered women. Because guessing can lead to unintended outcomes, ongoing analysis, collection of information, and the opportunity to modify positions are essential for responsible policy advocacy.

Like woman-defined individual advocacy, woman-defined policy advocacy, although aspiring to keep all battered women safe, is a pragmatic approach. Woman-defined policy advocacy deals with real options and resources and tries to make the most of them for battered women. It does not mean that the position taken or advocated will always be the best approach, but perhaps it is the best one available. The positions to take may be a choice between several problematic alternatives—each with some promise, each fraught with difficulties. Policy decisions and positions might change as new information is gathered, strategies are tested and evaluated, and new factors are considered.

A woman-defined approach to policy advocacy is guided by several core assumptions derived from work with individual battered women. Assumptions alone will not determine policy positions, however; decisions will also be affected by a combination of opportunity, resources, timing, politics, and power. The following core assumptions, summarized in Figure 9.1, are a starting point for developing a woman-defined policy analysis.

Acknowledge That Each
Battered Woman Is Unique

Preconceived uniform strategies or service-defined advocacy will not successfully respond to the uniqueness of battered women. For

Woman-defined policy advocacy should acknowledge that each battered woman is unique.

- Preconceived uniform strategies or service-defined advocacy will not successfully respond to the uniqueness of battered women.

Woman-defined policy advocacy should acknowledge and seek to address the range of batterer-generated risks that battered women face.

- A wide variety of options and resources should be available to battered women, providing strategies and responses that seek to address the risk of physical violence and all other batterer-generated risks.
- Each option should be as effective as possible.
- The limitations of a particular response should be acknowledged as part of the public policy dialogue, specifically to battered women.
- Responses to the range of batterer-generated risks should be multidisciplinary and collaborative.

Woman-defined policy advocacy should acknowledge and seek to address the range of life-generated risks that battered women face.

- Responses to battered women must acknowledge the reality of life-generated risks and incorporate strategies to address them in systemic responses to family violence.
- Responses to family violence should seek to minimize batterers' opportunities to manipulate life-generated risks to further their control of their partners.

Woman-defined policy advocacy should include strategies for battered women who stay in or return to their relationships, as well as battered women who have left or are planning to leave.

- Woman-defined policy advocacy and analysis should consider and incorporate the range of battered women's safety plans, including plans for staying.
- Responses to battered women should acknowledge and anticipate that women's analyses and plans will change and allow for that change.

Woman-defined policy advocacy should seek to ensure that battered women have access to individual woman-defined advocacy.

- The opportunity for such advocacy must exist.
- The potential for life-threatening violence must be identified, responded to, and balanced with the reality that not all battered women face this risk.
- The protection of battered mothers and children must be included as an integrated aspect of responding to battered women.
- The differing roles of battered women's advocates and other professionals responding to family violence should be clearly established and communicated.

Figure 9.1. Summary of Woman-Defined Policy Analysis Assumptions

example, a policy position that every battered woman whose partner is arrested will be given a protective order removing her partner from the home is a uniform and service-defined approach (protective orders for all). This approach does not respond to the many battered women who do not want or need a protective order or women who may face greater risks if a protective order is made. Conversely, policies and programs that acknowledge individual battered women's differences by providing a range of strategies and responses are more likely to be beneficial to more battered women.

Acknowledge and Seek to Address
the Range of Batterer-Generated Risks

First, each option should be as effective as possible. This does not mean every option will "end domestic violence," but rather will deliver the resources it was intended to provide. In other words, battered women can count on the options to accomplish what they were designed to accomplish.

Second, the limitations of a particular response should be acknowledged as part of the public policy dialogue. These limitations should also be communicated directly to battered women. This will more clearly identify the gaps in response, provide a more accurate view for both policymakers and battered women, and perhaps place less inappropriate responsibility on battered women themselves for having such poor choices.

Third, a wide variety of options and resources that seek to address the risk of physical violence and all other batterer-generated risks should be available to battered women. Acknowledging battered women's risk analysis means acknowledging that physical violence is not the only, or for some women even the primary, risk. Responses to family violence that focus exclusively on physical violence are important but limited. This does not mean that every agency must offer the entire spectrum of options. Responses to the range of batterer-generated risks should be multidisciplinary and collaborative, because each system is limited in what it can do. For example, a woman may find herself in criminal court, where the primary focus is on responding to physical violence, yet her primary risk is losing her means of financial support. The criminal court may be aware of the financial risk, but not have the means to address it. Therefore, the court should provide the woman with referrals and information about help regarding her financial concerns. Collaboration is part of an overall policy strategy to help battered women develop effective safety plans. Effective policy analysis would determine which agency could best provide particular options from the standpoint of battered women.

Child Protective Service

A child protection system protocol specifically requires the investigation and identification of domestic violence as one of a number of factors to consider when determining whether a child is at risk. The practice is to require that either the battered mother separates from her abusive partner or the children are removed from their home. The child protection workers will provide a referral to a local domestic violence shelter and tell each woman she should get a protective order.

Analysis. This child protection system is trying to respond to the risk that domestic violence might pose for children. Once the risk is identified, however, the system offers only one option: The battered mother must separate from her partner or have the children removed. The system does little to implement that option, providing only a referral and advice to get an order of protection. The system incorrectly assumes that children and their mothers will be safer if the mothers separate from their partners. Workers do not support or advocate for the mother, so even that one option is less likely to be effective. In addition, this child protection system does not work collaboratively with the local domestic violence project, but merely gives battered mothers a number to call. It is not clear whether the system acknowledges the limits of its response to other policymakers or the battered mothers involved with the system. The protocol states that the investigation and identification of domestic violence is an important goal, however, and therefore implies the system is "responding" to domestic violence.

Policy advocacy to enhance this system's response might include the development of a process that would ensure a more thorough investigation and assessment. This would more accurately determine which children are at risk because of domestic violence. The system would develop additional options for battered mothers, including options that address risks other than physical violence. For example, such options might include meeting the housing and financial needs of battered mothers who will lose their partners' support when they leave. In addition, policy advocates might seek a more effective implementation of all options, including support, information, and other advocacy for battered mothers seeking to protect themselves and their children. Another enhancement would be collaboration with the local domestic violence project and other systems responding to family violence. An acknowledgment of the limitations of the system's response to battered mothers could help individual safety planning, and acknowledgment to other policymakers would likely facilitate more meaningful and relevant changes to the system overall.

Acknowledge and Seek to Address
the Range of Life-Generated Risks

Policy work regarding life-generated risks must begin with the simple acknowledgment that those risks exist and are real barriers faced by battered women and others. Although simple in content, this acknowledgment may be difficult to achieve. Key players in a system may be unwilling to identify life-generated risks, particularly if the risks are caused by the system, such as discrimination. The acknowledgment of life-generated risks will help battered women by providing a more accurate picture of their lives and options. The acknowledgment alone is not enough, however. Strategies to reduce life-generated risks must be developed and included in family violence policies.

Policies that seek to address only batterer-generated risks provide an incomplete response to family violence and will fail to keep battered women and children safe. Life-generated risks will undermine the success of efforts that respond only to batterer-generated risks. Because life-generated and batterer-generated risks are intertwined, responses must be developed that address both. For example, the domestic violence shelter responding to batterer-generated risks must address risks such as poverty, home location, and discrimination. Similarly, the agency responding to poverty must address batterer-generated risks. The strategy to address all risks may be as simple as a referral, but it must be done sensitively and consistently, with an understanding of the connections among the issues for an individual woman. For example, responses to family violence should minimize a batterer's opportunities to manipulate life-generated risks to further his control of his partner.

Include Strategies for Battered Women
With Different Types of Plans

There are two aspects of this component of woman-defined policy analysis. First, woman-defined policy advocacy and analysis should consider and support the range of battered women's safety plans. Battered women's safety plans might involve protection strategies, along with long-range or short-term strategies for staying in or leaving the relationship. Policy positions responding to only one type of strategy, such as plans by battered women who have already left their relationships or are planning to leave immediately, will not respond to a significant number of battered women. This means anticipating that many battered women will remain in their relationships as they seek help or otherwise come in contact with service providers. The reality that leaving a relationship may not reduce a battered woman's risks must be integrated into options and strategies available to battered women. There are significant implications for this, including identifying current and new ways to keep women and children safer in an abusive relationship. Also, the plea of so many battered women, "please change him" must be part of the response, because strategies that try to change the batterer, although they may fail, may still be the best option for some battered women.

Second, responses to battered women should acknowledge and anticipate that their analyses and plans will change and allow for that change. Battered women's risk analyses and safety planning are fluid; decisions will change as hopes and fears shift, as the response is found to be effective or lacking, and as the women gather new information.

Seek to Ensure That Battered Women Have Access to Individual Woman-Defined Advocacy

Individual woman-defined advocacy responds to battered women's needs to regain control in their lives. It also increases the likelihood that advocates and battered women will share information that responds to women's risk analyses, enhances their present safety plans, and works within the realities of the women's lives and options. First, the opportunity for such advocacy must exist. There must be advocates who have the time, place, knowledge, skill, and protection of confidentiality to create partnerships with battered women. Second, the potential for life-threatening violence must be identified, responded to, and balanced with the reality that not all battered women face this risk. This is a difficult balance. Because the stakes are so high and the loss of life is so unacceptable, the tendency is to "err" on the side of caution. This makes sense. This response must be tempered with the understanding that many battered women do not face lethal violence, however. Third, the protection of battered mothers and children must be included as an integral aspect of advocacy with battered women. Fourth, as discussed in Chapter 8, "Toward a Woman-Defined Advocacy Environment," the differing roles of battered women's advocates and other professionals responding to family violence should be clearly identified.

Woman-Defined Advocacy as a Policy Process

Woman-defined policy development and implementation considers and integrates battered women's perspectives with those of advocates. This rather broad approach can guide, but will not by itself define, the "right" or "best" answers to the extremely difficult questions involved in policy work. Therefore, a process for developing policy positions is also necessary. This process is a way of building a supportive and creative structure for the policymakers—a call to gather information, to think, and to plan. A woman-defined policy process has elements similar to the process for individual advocacy.

Elements of a woman-defined policy process include the following:

- Provide woman-defined policy advocacy to further individual woman-defined advocacy and enhance safety for all battered women.
  - Gather information and determine who needs to be involved in the process.
  - Analyze and review the information gathered.
  - Develop a position based on the analysis and plan how to implement it.
  - Monitor and enhance the plan by continuing the information gathering, analysis, and strategizing.

The process will be determined by the time and resources available, the arena in which the policy advocacy will be offered, and the nature of the policy decision. If time or resources are limited, the process may be implemented in an informal, short-term way. With more time, the process may become more formal and detailed and span several months or years. Legislative advocacy often requires instantaneous decisions about particular policy positions; therefore, a process in the legislative arena would need to be available immediately and completed quickly. If potential legislative positions are planned and considered in advance, the instantaneous decision-making process will be more informed.

Where the advocacy is done and what the advocacy is about will also influence the process. For example, local policy advocacy about narrow issues, such as instituting a referral protocol between a police department and the battered women's shelter, will most likely involve a less extensive process than advocacy about a statewide position on mandatory arrest by police.

It is sometimes essential to "keep it simple" in policy work, providing broad, clear messages about the problem and the answers to that problem. A message of woman-defined advocacy is that family violence is complex and options for battered women and children's safety must respond to individual circumstances. Therefore, a particular challenge of woman-defined policy advocacy is conveying that complexity in simple terms. Advocates must also provide concrete solutions to the issues they raise and guide the policy response to this complexity.

Gather Information and Determine
Who Needs to Be Involved in the Process

The two threshold questions are what information should be gathered and how should the information be gathered. Ideally, the amount of information will reflect the nature of the policy decision. For example, if the policy advocacy is about a complex topic having far-reaching consequences for many battered women and other groups, more information will be needed to make decisions than for simple issues with narrower circumstances. For example, telecommunications issues are complex. The implementation of new technology, such as caller identification, may affect the privacy of everyone using the telephone and some battered women's physical safety as well. A lot of detailed information is necessary to consider such policy issues, including information about how the technology works, the forums in which telecommunications public policy decisions are made, and federal and state law.

Although the type of information will differ depending on the advocacy, two areas of information are necessary to gather in every instance: 1) To be woman-defined, policy advocacy must gather information about what battered women think about the issue and how the current policy position affects battered women and their children. Battered women will not be the only source of information; advocates and others involved with a particular policy will also have a valuable perspective about the effects of a policy. 2) Effective advocacy also requires a thorough understanding of the current system and policy. There is a reason current policies developed the way they did, and advocates need to understand why. This might include information about the system, the issues raised by the current policy and any proposed change in the policy, the key people who influence the system, how policies are implemented, the process to change current policies, and a sense of advocates' relative power to influence the process.

A part of the information gathering is considering who else needs to be involved in the process. This includes what types of groups, job functions, agencies, or disciplines need to be represented, and which individuals will actually be the representatives. For example, a project to develop a health care protocol will need representation from health care providers such as nurses, doctors, and social workers. Other representatives might include battered women, battered women's advocates, and any other groups that might be involved in the protocol, such as hospital security staff and law enforcement personnel.

How to Gather Information

Strategies for information gathering can vary dramatically. They can be ongoing or short-term; they can involve general documentation or relate to a specific project or need; they can be informal or more structured and complex. Such strategies, for example, include formal research and evaluation projects or program documentation, as well as focus groups, advisory councils, consultants and liaisons to particular communities, and discussions with women, advocates, or others in regular contact with battered women. Because time and resources are usually limited, gathering information will be most successful if it becomes an integrated part of advocates' work. In other words, it becomes the way the work is done.

Information gathering related to battered woman-defined policy analysis will have three primary sources: battered women, people who are involved in the various systems who work with these women, and written information, including research and documents. Collecting information from all three sources will be easiest and most useful if it is done regularly. Information from women about the current system and particular policies can be incorporated into a regular plan for documenting advocates' work. Appendix A, "Considerations for Information Gathering," provides a discussion of some ways to gather information and some of the issues to be addressed as information-gathering processes are designed.

Analyze and Review the Information Gathered

The questions and considerations that might be included in an analysis are almost limitless. In addition, information gathering from battered women will probably not point to a single clear "answer" or position, but rather identify the variety of interests to be balanced. There may be very difficult decisions to make with little time, incomplete information, and only a guess about the future effect of the decision. Although the nature of the policy advocacy and resources available will determine the extent and depth of analysis, it is helpful to develop, in advance, a list of questions to include in each analysis. The following questions are suggestions for that list.

What Are the Limits or Strengths of the Information Gathered?

In addition to all the issues listed in the previous section, a key consideration is the source of the information. If the information is about a particular group of people or agencies, are all the important subgroups included as sources of information? For example, if the information is supposed to be about all battered women, are women of color included? Are women who have decided for now to stay in their relationships included? Are battered women from the community included, not just women who went to the shelter? If the information is supposed to be about advocates, were all types of advocates included? In other words, these are questions about sampling, whether the sources of information were representative of the group as a whole.

When the information was gathered may also limit or strengthen its validity. For example, a public opinion poll conducted immediately after a well-publicized event, such as the domestic homicide of a public figure, may affect the way people answer questions about the frequency of domestic homicide or policies about gun control.

How Will the Policy Help or Hurt Battered Women?

Considering whether a policy will help or hurt battered women will necessarily lead to additional considerations, such as the following:

How will the policy be implemented? Policy implementation includes planning how to achieve the goals of the policy and then executing that plan. Policy analysis should look at both aspects. First consider how the implementation plan will be developed and what it will include, and then how the executed plan will affect battered women. This analysis goes beyond considering what the policy is supposed to do, to thinking about what it actually will do. Even policies with good intentions can lead to negative consequences for battered women when implemented. Policy analysis must try to anticipate and weigh such outcomes.

Welfare and Domestic Violence

A state policy is that "applicants for welfare assistance should receive information about domestic violence services."

Analysis of the planning for the implementation of this policy would include the following questions about the process: What is the decision-making process, including who has the ultimate authority to make the decisions? Will it be the agency administering the welfare program? If so, who in the agency will make the decisions and what process will she or he use? Is there an opportunity for advocacy in that process? Will there be an opportunity for battered women's feedback as the policy is implemented?

Analysis would also include the following questions about the content of the plan: What information will be provided to applicants? What form will the information take? Will it be oral, written, and in what language? When will applicants be given the information? Who will actually provide the information—a welfare intake worker? Which domestic violence services will be included? How will the services be described? Do the services have enough resources to respond to the potentially increased demand? What will happen if they do not?

Once a plan is made about how the information will be provided to battered women, advocates should analyze the execution of the plan in detail. This means thinking through each step of the process from the perspective of the battered woman experiencing it. For example, the implementation plan for the above policy might be to screen all applicants for assistance for domestic violence to refer them to services. On the face of it, this proposal seems reasonable: Identify domestic violence victims to refer them to services. There are many details to consider, however, such as are the setting and method of screening conducive for disclosure of domestic violence information? What is the tone of the questioner? Can the conversation be overheard by others? How would a battered woman perceive the reason for the questions? If she does disclose, how much information will she be expected or allowed to disclose? What is the likely response of the questioner? What if the woman needs support or other intervention? Could there be consequences for a victim who "lies" when she is asked about domestic violence? How might the identification of domestic violence be used against her? For example, in a custody case, disclosure might have implications for child protection involvement or retaliation from her abusive partner.

An alternative to the above screening policy would be to provide all applicants for assistance with information about domestic violence services. This universal notification approach would allow women to decide whether to disclose domestic violence information, for what purposes, and to whom.

How will different groups of battered women be affected? It is impossible to consider how each policy will affect every group of battered women. Just identifying the groups can be challenging. In addition to commonly used categories such as ethnicity, woman-defined analysis will consider new ones. These groups might include battered women who stay in their relationships, leave their relationship with the intention of returning, leave permanently, have long-range plans to leave, and will not or cannot use the police. There are many ways to define groups; how they are defined will significantly affect whether policies are seen as helpful or harmful and to whom.

When analyzing the effects of a policy on different groups of battered women, advocates must include a review of life-generated risks. Particular policies may raise the dangers of life-generated risks. For example, a response to family violence that eliminates or reduces the family's income will have a particularly harsh effect on poor battered women and children. Policy analysis of life-generated risks should consider the response of the system itself. If the system in which an advocate is advocating discriminates or responds ineffectively to particular groups of women, then this reality must be considered and countered in the policy developed.

Another aspect of this analysis is whether the policy will allow or facilitate batterers' manipulation of life-generated risks to further their control. For example, a state may pass a new policy to remove children from their homes when a parent is arrested for domestic violence. Batterers could use this policy as a threat to keep their partners from disclosing the abuse or calling the police.

A particular policy may help or harm some battered women and have no effect on others.

Health Care Provider Policy

A policy requires all health care providers to call the police when treating an injury they believe to be caused by domestic violence. Dr. Smith followed the policy and had the police called while she was stitching Julie's lip. The police came to the doctor's office and questioned Dr. Smith, Julie, and Julie's partner, who was in the waiting room. They arrested Julie's partner and took him to the police station.

Analysis of whether this policy will help or hurt Julie would depend on her risk analysis and safety plans. If police involvement might lead to negative consequences for Julie, such as retribution by her partner, the loss of employment, or the loss of privacy, then it would hurt Julie and women in similar situations. If, however, Julie was looking for an opportunity to get away from her partner and the arrest will provide that chance, then it might help her and women like her. Therefore, the health care provider might adopt a general policy of contacting law enforcement, with different protocols for the different situations that may arise. These protocols might include immediate contact with police with the patient's permission, providing the patient with information on how to contact the police and the likely consequences of calling them, documenting injuries for potential future prosecution or legal action, and no documentation or contact if that may increase the patient's danger.

Do battered women have a meaningful opportunity to choose among options and influence how they will be provided? It is important to get the system to respond as effectively as possible while providing the opportunity for an individual woman's plans to influence the response. This does not mean the individual woman will always get what she wants or needs or that she will make the final decision. There are situations in which the policy goals and the individual woman's plans will match, and there will be times when they will not. Woman-defined individual advocacy will provide additional options to women when the policy goals and her safety plans do not match.

Develop a Position Based on the
Analysis and Plan How to Implement It

Policy advocacy cannot stop with policy analysis. The analysis must lead to a policy agenda. To develop an agenda, advocates need to identify and prioritize the key issues affecting battered women. Advocates must take particular policy positions proactively to move their agenda forward.

Once advocates are established participants in the policy process, they will be asked and expected to make decisions about particular issues and proposals initiated by others. For example, an advocate might be asked, "Is it a good idea for the state to create a computer database of all convicted batterers and make it available to the public?" After doing whatever analysis time allows (sometimes no more than a minute or two), the advocate needs to respond. Without a response, the analysis from battered women's perspectives will be lost.

Given the many uncertainties and challenges of policy analysis, it can be frightening to take a position. There is always the possibility the position has unintended negative consequences or is otherwise somehow "wrong." Advocates can take some comfort from the fact that policy advocacy is an ongoing process. A policy decision should not stop the analysis; when the decision is not the best one, advocates can acknowledge its weakness and modify the position.

What Policy Can Be Achieved?

To answer this question, advocates must consider the context of politics and power in which policy advocacy is done. For example, an elected official may agree with a particular position, but tell the advocate he will not publicly support it until after an election. Alternatively, an elected official may support a particular position because she thinks it will help her get elected, but have no intention of supporting the actual implementation of the policy. Taking a position that is achievable rather than ideal is a part of policy advocacy. Determining which compromises to make can be difficult.

Mandatory Arrest

Battered women's policy advocates gather information and complete a thorough analysis of mandatory arrest for family violence crimes. They decide that mandatory arrest will help more battered women than it will hurt, provided that advocacy is available for each woman whose partner is arrested. The advocates' state legislature wants to pass a mandatory arrest law, but has taken a position that no new programs, such as advocacy, will be added to the state budget. The advocates know there will be no compromise on the budget issue. These advocates face the difficult decision about compromising the advocacy aspect of mandatory arrest. As part of the decision, the advocates must return to their analysis and consider how mandatory arrest might help or hurt women, and which women will be helped or hurt, when there is little or no advocacy available.

It is necessary in policy work to prioritize certain goals and initiatives. This focuses the work and helps simplify the message. Prioritization can also make very important issues invisible, however. For example, if batterer-generated risks are the priority, life-generated risks may be ignored. Advocates need to be aware of all the issues and ensure that important issues are not completely lost in the policy dialogue. Even if the focus is on one area, advocates can still articulate the range of concerns and how they affect battered women.

Plan How to Implement the Policy

Knowing where you want to go is just part of policy advocacy; knowing how you are going to get there is just as important. Planning will guide how the policy advocacy will proceed. An implementation plan might be designed to pursue a policy position affirmatively, or to respond defensively if others pursue a particular position. In addition, the plan may simply be to "let it happen" and not take any action in support of or against a position. Planning might be an informal discussion and decision or a detailed work or action plan.

Implementations should be feasible. A feasible plan is based on accurate assumptions. For example, a plan to change the training curriculum for a local hospital may be based on the assumption that the administrator of the hospital will support the effort. The assumed position of the administrator should be confirmed as part of the planning process. Another check on feasibility is assessing the amount of time and resources needed to put the plan into action. Are the time lines realistic? Who will do the work? Do advocates have the resources and skills they need to be successful? If not, how will the additional resources and skills be acquired? If the plan is not feasible, then it is important to consider the consequences of not proceeding, delaying the implementation, or proceeding in a more limited way. If these consequences are unacceptable, advocates should try to shift resources to that policy area to make the plan feasible.

Monitor and Enhance the Plan by Continuing the Information Gathering, Analysis, and Planning

Policy advocacy should be seen as an ongoing and fluid process. Key factors in policy advocacy, such as information, resources, ability to influence outcomes, and the effect of current policies on battered women, are always in a state of flux. Advocacy must identify and respond to the changes. Ongoing monitoring of the implementation of a particular policy is especially important, because implementation will have a direct effect on battered women and their children. A formal policy and the actual practice can differ. For example, a particular prosecutor may exclude battered women defendants with self-defense claims from her proprosecution policy. A different prosecutor implementing the same policy may not exclude such cases. One way to make it easier to respond to the ever-changing nature of policy advocacy is to build into the implementation plan the opportunity and expectation of review and modification. For example, part of a protocol for a child protection system's response to domestic violence might include the quarterly review of the protocol by all the key players involved. These meetings would reflect the expectation that the protocol may change and provide an opportunity for battered women's advocates to participate.

Whether advocates have the opportunity to monitor and enhance policies will be determined by their credibility and influence with key decision makers. Access to the process; high-quality, thoughtful participation in that process; and collaboration with others involved will help advocates establish credibility and influence. Access, participation, and collaboration are interconnected. Collaboration will facilitate access, quality participation will help build collaboration, and access makes participation possible. The establishment of task forces, coordinating councils, or other advisory groups can facilitate advocate collaboration and access. Advocates need to pay close attention to the purpose, structure, resources, authority, and jurisdiction of such groups to determine their use in advancing a policy agenda. Furthermore, high-quality, thoughtful participation requires preparation. Advocates must be prepared to inform decision makers about the issues, apply that information to the current context, and present that information in a compelling format, whether oral or written. Such preparation may demand that advocates read, learn, think, and write.

Conclusion

Policy advocacy can be a messy undertaking. There can be widely differing views on what is "right" or "wrong," time lines can be short, information can be unavailable or incomplete, advocacy resources can be limited, and the stakes can be high. In addition, policy advocacy is typically done in a forum in which battered women's advocates are not in power. Success can be elusive. Even if advocates were sure of what policy would be best for battered women, there would be no guarantee that the policy could be achieved. Sometimes policy advocacy focuses on preventing "bad" policies from happening, rather than working to initiate a "good" policy. Compromising a position is often the "best" that can be achieved. Yet, battered women's policy advocates must continue to take action while keeping the vision. Ultimately, policy advocacy is a long-range safety plan for all battered women, one that will be ongoing and ever-changing, but relentless in its movement forward.

10

Conclusion

The woman-defined advocacy model described in this book, like battered women's safety plans, is based on current information, analysis, and experience. Application in different settings with diverse battered women will enrich and refine the model. This has been our experience in developing the model. We view it as an essential part of the process to provide battered women with the best advocacy possible. Whatever changes that process brings, the current model of individual and systemic woman-defined advocacy is likely to have immediate and potentially far-reaching implications.

The deliberate process of understanding battered women's perspectives and integrating advocates' knowledge and analysis will lead to more practical, reality-based responses to family violence. Understanding battered women's risk analyses will push advocates' own analysis beyond a focus on physical violence to consider all batterer-generated risks fully. Quick fixes and one-size-fits-all solutions will be replaced with long-term strategies more responsive to the diversity and complexity of each battered woman's needs. These strategies will provide battered women with better options.

Separation will no longer be seen as the only real answer to domestic violence. Hiding women will become just another option, and no longer the primary focus of advocacy. Advocates will respect and understand battered women's needs and desire to stay in their relationships. An implication of this is a greater emphasis on work to end men's violent behavior. Advocates will try to "change" the batterers because—as battered women so often tell us—this is what will reduce their risks.

Advocates' view and description of battered women will become more accurate and complete. Advocates will see and comprehend the incredible strength and creativity of battered women as they try to keep themselves and their children safe. Yet advocates will also see and be more candid about the weaknesses—when their risk analyses are not accurate and when safety plans for children are ineffective. Neither superwomen nor pathetic victims, battered women will be seen and described as real people facing very difficult situations, having limited options, and making tough choices.

Advocates' view of advocacy will also change. The work will be defined no longer by the services provided but by the partnerships developed with battered women. Advocates will have a more accurate view of what they can do to protect women and children. Advocates will become partners in safety planning, serving as listener, guide, liaison, clarifier, information source, and strategist. Battered women will have greater access to advocacy.

The conscious inclusion of life-generated risks in risk analyses will lead advocates to consider a broader range of issues and work toward more comprehensive solutions. The mission to end batterers' violence will be placed in the context of larger issues, such as poverty and discrimination based on race, ethnicity, or other characteristics. Advocates will expand their understanding of how batterers use life-generated risks to further their control. Advocacy will then include efforts to achieve economic justice, end racism and other discrimination, and respond to the range of life-generated risks.

The broader approach to advocacy will change what advocates consider to be "the work" and how they organize themselves to do it. In part, this means the work of advocates will include systemic advocacy. Advocates must build on the important criminal legal system initiatives, such as the Violence Against Women Act, arrest and prosecution initiatives, and court and community-based advocacy to develop a more comprehensive and integrated response to family violence. As advocates try to do more in more areas, they will need to collaborate. Turf battles and fights over who are the "real experts" on family violence must give way to open lines of communication, coordinated approaches, and respect and value for each player's contribution to ending violence against women.

None of this will be easy. The status quo is difficult to overcome. There are sometimes long histories of conflict. Funding is limited, and competition for scarce resources can divide and divert energies. Like the battered women with whom they work, advocates may need to develop long-range strategies for using every resource they can find, stay in the work, and try to change the social environment. Woman-defined advocates will amplify the voices of battered women and work in partnership with them to think and plan.

Appendix A

Considerations for Information Gathering

Ongoing Program Documentation

Ongoing program documentation is a deliberate gathering and recording of specific information about what the program does, who does it, and with whom. Documenting work is often seen by advocates as superfluous, because it is a requirement imposed by funders who may not understand the work and who insist on "stats" that record numbers of people and services that do not seem meaningful. Program documentation is a useful tool, however, when it is based on an understanding of the work; in fact, good information is essential to effective woman-defined advocacy. It can help advocates learn more about the diversity of battered women's needs and resources, their community experiences as they seek help and make connections, the program's real strengths and weaknesses, gaps in the community's system of services and other responses, and other issues. Such information is important to have just for program self-appraisal and improvement. It can also provide the basis for policy analysis and community change. In addition, such information is valuable to share with other programs so they can learn from both good and bad experiences, and not have to "reinvent the wheel."

The most important principles for ongoing program documentation and for shorter-term information gathering as part of special projects are similar, and similar to some of the tenets of basic advocacy.

The Information Collected Must Not Jeopardize
Women's Physical or Emotional Safety

All identifying information must be kept out of sight and securely locked. Information that could have negative consequences, if revealed, should either not be collected, be stored without names attached, or be retained only as long as it remains essential for work with the woman and then destroyed, or another strategy should be developed. Legal consultation about applicable precedents regarding privacy and confidentiality can help establish the balance between privacy and the need to gather information. In addition, questions that are likely to be upsetting should be asked only when a woman is prepared for them and when emotional support resources (such as friends, close family members, or trained counselors) are available.

The Information Should Be Collected Respectfully

When information is collected hastily, just to complete necessary paperwork, it tells women that the information they are giving is not important. The best information is likely to be provided when there is enough time to listen, when women can use their own words, and neither the woman nor the advocate is distracted by other concerns. For example, this might mean that some parts of an intake interview can wait until the woman is calmer, she has had a chance to eat or is not distracted by crying children, and the advocate is not answering the telephone or attending to other duties.

The Information Should Be Collected With Respect for
Women's Unique Situations and Individual Differences

Women should be given an opportunity to explain their experiences, and, when it is safe to do so, that information should be recorded, along with the more succinct check mark in the appropriate box. In general, information that is collected by choosing among response categories developed by funders or researchers ("checking the boxes") will not provide enough of the kind of information that can help us learn more about the full range of women's experiences and the ways they make sense of their situations. Complete information about battered women's experiences and strategies is still limited, and is essential for advancing woman-defined advocacy and policy analysis.

The Information Should Include Women's Strengths
and Resources, in Addition to Their Needs

This information, too, is central to advocacy, but is often over-looked as part of documentation. Woman-defined advocacy will include obtaining information from women about their strategies for the short- and longer-term future relationship with their abusive partner (strategies for staying or leaving) and protecting their children. It would not be complicated to add this to the information that is collected from all women. More of this type of information will be helpful for agency planning and policy decisions, and contribute to a more accurate and complex public understanding of battered women.

Depending on the type of program, ongoing documentation can include the following kinds of information: background information that may affect a battered woman's options and decision making, such as her age, education, number of children, work experience, and her assessment of both batterer-generated and life-generated risks; her needs, concerns, and immediate goals; other agencies and resources she has used; whether or not she found those options helpful and how; the services offered and provided by the advocate; and the woman's reactions to those services. Part of ongoing program documentation, then, may include regular "checking in" with a woman about her experiences with the services she receives.

Although counting services does not provide a full picture of what an advocate or agency does or their usefulness to a woman, counting may be useful for some purposes; it can show the effect of a change in policy, for example, if the patterns of services change. Such documentation will help identify some of the strengths and weaknesses of different types of intervention. It will also provide basic, ongoing data about some aspects of what battered women think about the current system and set of policies. It does not need to be complicated. It can consist of a simple log of contacts with other agencies and what happened with the contacts: what did they do, what was accomplished, what problems the woman encountered.

In addition to this kind of program documentation, procedures to gather regular feedback can be very useful. Talking with women just before they leave a program can provide information about what they found especially helpful (or not). Agencies that contact women after they have left the program to see how they are doing have often found such efforts worthwhile for reconnecting with women who again need services or support, reinforcing the message of continuing concern and accessibility, and learning more about women's longer-term strategies for addressing the abuse in their lives.

A different kind of approach to gathering regular feedback could involve periodic meetings with battered women. For example, information could be provided about aspects of a particular policy or proposal, and the women's reactions could be documented. Similar meetings could also be organized with networks of service providers or other agencies involved in the work. This can be an invaluable strategy for collecting policy-relevant information and strengthening collaborative relationships at the same time. Again, documentation does not need to be complicated; it can include simply the people or organizations represented, the topic, the issues raised, any problems identified, and solutions discussed.

Incorporating information gathering into "the way the work is done" means not only regular documentation, but understanding its importance for decision making of all sorts. It is important to evaluate every new policy, program, or approach that is tried to find out if it is helpful or harmful, how it is helpful or harmful, and for whom. Regular, ongoing documentation will usually make that evaluation much easier and more effective, because it will be possible to compare before-and-after information.

Advocates themselves can be a source of information. An advocate's experiences and reactions may be shared by other people. If an advocate feels uncomfortable with the atmosphere in a particular agency, it is conceivable that battered women could feel uncomfortable there as well. If staff at another agency are curt or rude when an advocate calls to make a referral, that may reflect how they approach the women who come to them for help. It can be useful to have a formal practice to record these experiences or observations systematically. Over time, they can accumulate a powerful picture, and do not take much time to document.

Specific Projects or Issues

As part of the policy analysis and advocacy process, specific issues or occasions will require information that is not part of ongoing program documentation. The type of strategy for gathering this information will depend on the time and resources available and the questions that need to be answered. Sometimes it will be most efficient and feel safest to talk with interviewees in groups; they can learn from each other and feed off each others' ideas. Group experiences can also reinforce that people are not alone, so the research process can be empowering as well. Sometimes the topics will be potentially sensitive, and many participants will not want to talk in front of a group. If it is important to hear answers to all questions from everyone, it may work better to talk separately. In addition, different issues will arise with different sources of information.

Issues When Battered Women Are the Source of Information

If battered women will be approached to gather information for a specific purpose or research project, several general issues should be thought through, including those related to respect for women's uniqueness and safety. Thinking about all these issues will be more productive if battered women are involved or at least consulted during the process.

How Will Women Be Informed About the Goals of the Research?

This should include an explanation of the reasons for the questions and the kinds of questions women will be asked. This is an essential part of informed consent included in the "protection of human subjects" for all research, and is especially important for battered women. The explanations must be understandable and available in the woman's primary language.

How Will the Research Ensure That Women's Participation Is Voluntary?

Women must understand that there will be no consequence to them if they choose not to answer the questions. For example, women often think that they can be denied shelter or that advocates will be less helpful to them if they are "uncooperative."

How Will the Confidentiality of Women's Answers Be Maintained?

What women say should not be revealed to anyone without their explicit consent, except as part of describing responses anonymously. If there are questions about child abuse, the women must be informed that if they reveal abuse, it will be reported to the child protection agency.

How Will the Research Ensure the Questions Asked Do Not Put Women at Physical or Emotional Risk?

This means that support systems should be in place if questions are difficult, and women should be assured that questions can be stopped at any time. It also means the site where questions are asked must be safe. It is useful to review a safety plan for the situation before the conversation or interview begins. It can include strategies for responding to her batterer if he appears unexpectedly. For example, if the conversation takes place by telephone, the plan can include a phrase the woman can use to signal danger before she ends the call, and an understanding about how and when the conversation can be resumed.

How Will the Research Ensure the Questions Are Necessary?

It is important to understand the goals of the questions clearly before beginning, and be sure the questions will elicit answers. Extra, unnecessary questioning of women is not respectful of their time or privacy and should be avoided. It is sometimes tempting to add just a few extra questions "since we're talking anyway" because the questions are interesting and would not take too much more time.

It is also important, however, that questions are asked in enough detail so the answers can be interpreted appropriately. For example, asking a woman only where she is going to live when she leaves a shelter is unlikely to provide enough information about her plans to be useful. "Return to the batterer at exit" is often interpreted as an indication of the woman's weakness or the shelter's failure. Instead, this may be part of her longer-term plan for leaving, it can be part of her strategy to enhance her power and leverage in the relationship, and it can have many other meanings in the context of the individual woman's life and plans.

How Will the Research Ensure That the Format of the Questions Gathers the Desired Information?

In general, if advocates want to understand something, the questions should allow women to explain, describe, or offer ideas in their own words. If advocates want information about how many women do or think something in particular, then it is important to figure out exactly what needs to be (and can be) counted. Both of these types of information can be valuable. For example, an advocate may want to know how many women have had particular types of good or bad experiences with the police or therapists. The advocate may also want to know how women felt about or understood a particular type of police response or therapeutic approach. It is often helpful to ask both the counting (quantitative) and the explanatory or descriptive (qualitative) types of questions; they can provide a powerful picture together.

The best approach to addressing these issues is to test the questions first. Researchers call this part of the process a *pilot* or *trial*. This is not as difficult as it might sound, and it can be enormously helpful to avoid misunderstandings and other problems. It simply means that once a draft of questions has been developed, they should be tried out with a small group of battered women. It is important that the women involved at this stage include women who are as diverse with respect to education, race and ethnicity, age, social class, and other important characteristics as the women the advocate plans to include. A pilot involves asking the questions and asking explicitly if the questions are clear or how they were understood. The phrasing of the questions can then be changed so that women understand them in the way intended and do not feel they show a bias or judgment the questioner had not considered.

In particular, testing should identify the meanings women attach to particular words or phrases. Battered women and advocates may associate different meanings to such words as *battered, abuse,* or *violence.* Many women who are physically assaulted regularly by their partners, for example, do not think of themselves as "battered women"; there are also regional, local, class, and ethnic differences in terminology. It is important to use the words that women understand in the way the questioner intended.

Testing must go beyond the specific words used to consider whether the way questions are phrased implies judgments about women's behavior or assumptions about women's options. Women experience different realistic options, depending on their race and ethnicity, economic circumstances, age, and sexual orientation, among other factors. For example, a question such as "Why didn't you call the police when he hit you?" could seem to imply the judgment that calling the police was the best response, when in fact it may not be for some women for a variety of reasons. A question that starts "why" demands an explanation and may put women on the defensive. An alternative question on this topic is, "What did you think might happen if you called the police?" This question is neutral, and gathers information on the woman's thought process instead of eliciting a defensive rationale.

Issues When an Agency Is the Source of Information

In addition to the issues listed above, attention must be paid to the agency's decision-making structure. Who needs to give permission for the research? What authority is necessary to gain access to the agency's staff and information? What confidentiality protocols must be followed? When approaching an agency, a researcher must be candid and accurate about the research, the burden it may place on the agency's resources, and the process for analysis and distribution of the information. Researchers should also consider that an agency's staff may be reluctant to answer questions for a variety of reasons, including past experience with research. Political considerations will also affect the agency's level of participation.

Information gathered about an agency that is useful to woman-defined policy analysis can include the following: Does the agency screen for family violence? What options and resources does the agency provide? What eligibility criteria does the agency use? What referrals does the agency make? Does the agency do outreach and to whom? Does the agency facilitate women's participation in exploring their options and deciding what to do? What is the agency's policy and practice for sharing information about the women it serves?

Appendix B 🖋

Building the Model:
The Connecticut Experience

Much of the experience that prompted the development of the woman-defined advocacy model occurred in the criminal legal system. In the aftermath of Tracy Thurman's successful lawsuit against a city police department, Connecticut's governor formed a task force to study responses to domestic violence across the state. The result was a new state law that aimed to take domestic violence incidents more seriously than before: to provide support to victims and immediate intervention for batterers. Connecticut was one of the first states to adopt such legislation.

Connecticut's Family Violence Prevention and Response Act was passed and implemented in 1986. Among its provisions were mandatory arrest with probable cause, arraignment on the next court day following arrest, the clearly specified option of protective orders, a pretrial offender education program for first-time misdemeanor arrestees, and the creation of a new position: the *family violence victim advocate* (FVVA). The law was more comprehensive than those found in other states; it required people who hold court positions with quite different responsibilities to confer and collaborate in decisions about domestic violence cases. It also required that statistical data on arrest, court referral, and court dispositions be collected and reported annually to the legislature for the first 5 years.

The law was implemented with collaborative oversight as well. A statewide committee was formed to monitor the law and to identify problems and their solutions. The committee also identified needed revisions in the law and shared statistical data. Subcommittees on training, medical reporting, and research and evaluation were formed and became active. The state has a tradition of valuing research as a tool for assessing the effectiveness of new initiatives and for guiding program improvement.

A study of the implementation of the law, with a focus on the specialized advocates, provided support for concerns raised at meetings of the interdisciplinary monitoring committee. Advocates reported that police too often arrested both or all people present when they responded to a domestic violence call. In addition, they often neglected to tell women about the advocacy and shelter services available to them. Through a police training project, a new curriculum was developed that focused on investigative and interviewing techniques and the necessity of police providing information and referral.

As important, the study provided an early source of concern about advocacy. Most of that concern related to the unprecedented and sudden increase in the volume of cases, the (often marginal) status of advocates in court, and limitations on the available remedies and services (see Lyon & Mace, 1989, 1991). In open-ended interviews with the advocates about their work, half made a distinction between what the battered women they saw in court wanted and what they "really" needed. Nearly half of the advocates described women's desires for support and understanding, as in the following excerpt:

> They want to talk to someone who understands what's happening. They want to know what's causing it, and how to make it end. Someone who believes them, and will support what they want to do. Someone who won't tell them what to do or that they necessarily have to leave the relationship.

Close to half of the FVVAs commented that the women wanted the abuse to end, but did not want to end the relationship. In contrast, about half of the advocates said that what the women "really needed" was independence, self-esteem, and programs to help make independence a reality.

The advocates were also asked about the biggest obstacles and greatest frustrations they experienced in their work with battered women. The biggest problems they noted were the lack of criminal sanctions available to the courts. This was followed closely by the women's ambivalence, especially about ending the relationship, as a source of advocate frustration. The next most common frustration, and one of the most frequent of the FVVA recommendations for changes in the job, related to advocates' lack of time to spend with the women. Several described what they called the "10-minute rap" that they customarily gave to the women they saw in court. Basically, the "rap" provided information about the law and the court process and explored women's options for protective orders.

This early experience with the new law illustrates how easily service-defined advocacy can evolve as the predominant model, even among people who have great concern about family violence and commitment to working with battered women. When the volume of cases increases and the available resources do not, service providers are more likely to focus their time and attention on the people who will most readily take advantage of what is offered. When the time available to spend with battered women decreases, advocates are more likely to focus their efforts on connecting women with the most accessible services. In this way, the services come to define the intervention strategies. These patterns were documented in an observational study of the court process.

This second study investigated the ways that family violence cases were handled in one large urban court. This study was prompted in part by findings from the interviews with advocates that the case-handling process in some court locations did not fully include the FVVAs and did not incorporate contact with battered women in the early stages. The goals of the study included understanding the actual court process and identifying protocols needed to help it operate more responsively.

The advocates and other personnel in this court expressed frustration with the battered women they encountered and with the failure of the court system to address their needs adequately. They discussed the women accepting responsibility for the abuse, their "denial," their desire to maintain the relationship, and the FVVAs' perception of the danger the women faced. Some court staff voiced their anger at the women for not leaving their relationship with the batterer and not being fully cooperative with protective orders. One advocate described her dilemma, and her recognition of the effect of service-defined advocacy (without using that term), particularly poignantly:

> We have only a few things to offer victims. So what we have to do is fit them into these slots, get them to accept what we have, transform their lives, and be grateful. If they don't, we imply they deserve to be assaulted again.

Overall, accumulated local studies of court and battered women's responses to their court experience demonstrated that when there was contact between women and the advocates,[1] it was most often brief and consisted of information provided by advocates to women, rather than an exchange. Information focused on the "remedies" available in court. Advocates often spent more of their limited time warning women about the dangerous potential for escalating violence than they did trying to understand the women's plans. Further contact was seldom initiated by the women, and in subsequent follow-up interviews, the women often could not distinguish the advocates from the other court staff they had talked to on the day of arraignment.

These court observations and interviews also provided a clear reminder that "real" battered women are diverse, with widely varying experiences, needs, hopes, and perspectives on their situations. The popular images of the "perfect" victim, or the battered woman who just needs a little support to transform her life, or the woman whose primary issue or concern is the violence in her life, were not supported in the court context. The lives of real people are messier and more complex than neatly constructed images (even when those images are grim).

The contrast between real women's lives and the organization of services was also found outside court. Information about local shelter rules and procedures revealed that some facilities had developed practices that discouraged some women from returning. For example, in some places, women who made efforts to contact their abusive partner were reprimanded (due to shelter safety concerns) and sometimes asked to leave. In other programs, the women who left shelters to return to their partners were not permitted to return for at least 6 months. As elsewhere, the language of shelter staff and court advocates became peppered with reference to the women's "minimization" and "denial" as ways of understanding their behavior.[2]

The law had brought thousands of battered women into contact with the court and with some information about resources available to them that many would not otherwise have obtained. The brief contact, however, often consisted of information that went from the advocate to the woman in unfamiliar language, under frightening and confusing circumstances. Follow-up interviews with women showed that many (certainly not all) of them did not leave with the feeling that their needs and concerns had been understood, or that they now had a new ally to whom they could usefully return in the future.[3]

This was the context for the development of the woman-defined safety planning model. The term *safety planning* was used initially to describe the process because it was a familiar and accessible term for advocates. Trainers hoped to build on what advocates already knew and did in their work. Further, *safety* was conceived in its broadest sense; it was not confined to immediate, physical safety. Similarly, *planning* was approached broadly and naturally; it was not confined to narrow, preconceived steps.

The model was first presented formally as a pilot in an intense day-long training. That first training began with what came to be known as the "marbles exercise," in which advocates were asked a series of questions by the trainer, who responded to their answers in ways that ranged from bureaucratic or noncommittal to curt and judgmental. The purpose of the exercise was to demonstrate how victims often feel in a court setting: powerless, subject to questions, stereotypic assumptions, and judgments about private areas of their lives from people who listen only partially, trying to guess the "right" answers that will lead to the help and responses they want. At first, some of the advocates were angry at the trainer, until the discussion after the exercise, when they understood its point. It was a powerful introduction to communication difficulties between advocates and battered women in court and other bureaucratic settings. The training also covered many of the basic elements of what emerged as the woman-defined advocacy model, which were then conceived as four steps: understanding the woman's perspective, assessing risk, building on the woman's plan, and reviewing and implementing the plan.

Based on evaluations, the training was subsequently expanded to 2 days, separated by at least a week. In addition, the marbles exercise was modified, and sections were added to include more time on jargon, sexual violence, and advocates' experiences trying the model.

Four years later, some advocates who took part in these early training sessions still had their marbles, to remind themselves how women can feel in these circumstances. Comments about the training and the model on evaluation forms completed over the course of a year demonstrate what the advocates saw as the primary changes the model required. The first question asked if there was "anything about the approach described in the training that stands out as different from what you have been doing." Seventy-eight percent of the advocates trained in the first year found differences in at least parts of the approach. Many advocates responded with a variation on "not assuming the woman wants to leave." One acknowledged her previous "tendency of telling battered women to get a protective order or restraining order without listening to their real fears and that a possibility or option is to stay with the abuser." Another observed, "This is the first time I've heard safety planning include her resources, hopes, and fears, and her view of the abuse." Yet another described this difference: "Putting *her* first; prioritizing her needs over my desire for statistical information." Yet another advocate responded to her early use of the model with relief: "I've always felt 100% responsible for the victim's safety. I don't any more, because I can work with victims more closely so they can come up with their own safety planning."

The first times the training was offered, the trainers held follow-up supervision meetings with advocates to review their experiences using the model. Advocates reported that they felt a combination of relief and concern when they used the model: relief at not being responsible for the women, and concern because they sometimes thought they should be responsible and/or were not supportive of the choices the women often made. Nonetheless, they acknowledged that the women had the right to make their own choices. Over time, many observed that they had begun to receive more calls and visits from the women with whom they had used the model than they had received with the old approach. Clearly, the women were becoming more likely to perceive the advocates as potentially helpful resources, and the advocates began to redefine success in their work.

As the model has been adopted and refined over the course of nearly 5 years, several features of the approach and the process have been especially notable.

Ongoing evaluation and analysis of the training and use of the model have contributed to successive refinements. Listening to both women and advocates has been a vital part of the process.

Finding the right balance between presenting the model as something "new" and "what we already do" has sometimes been challenging. Initially, training emphasized the approach as familiar so it would not be threatening. Some advocates then felt that all they needed to do to incorporate the model was to talk with women about their "partner" or "husband" instead of their "batterer" or "the defendant." Subsequent training has also emphasized the importance of making no assumptions or judgments, but taking the time to draw out the wom- en's own plans, hopes, strategies, and fears to develop a richer under- standing of their perspectives. Later training has also focused more attention on the need for advocates to "let go" of their (unrealistic) sense of responsibility for the safety of every woman they work with.

As successive training occurred, the importance of the model in the context of race and ethnicity and social class issues became clearer. Listening to women without making assumptions or judgments about their choices and alternatives is necessary for effective advocacy, yet sometimes difficult for some middle-class Anglo women to do. Advocates of color have been especially supportive and responsive to the model in training.

In response to advocates' concerns, the model itself has shifted. Initially, the advocates' role was too passive; it urged them to listen to women and craft an approach based almost purely on what the women wanted. Subsequently, the model has become a partnership that draws more fully on the advocates' skills and experiences as well. This more balanced, integrated approach emerged partly from advocates' concerns about potential lethality and about risks to children. The model now tries to identify boundaries, when the advocates' responsibilities may differ from "what the woman wants."

Over time, training on the woman-defined safety planning model was expanded. First, it was offered to shelter advocates and other staff who worked outside the legal system. Later, it was offered to other legal system staff, including generic victim advocates and the "family relations" counselors who work in court with the specialized family violence victim advocates. Some of the basic principles have also been shared in training with judges and prosecutors. This training has been a key part of spreading the model and understanding the complexities of battered women's experience and decision making. It has also reinforced the importance of respecting women's choices and maximizing their options as part of the legal system's response.

As the audience for training in the safety planning model diversified, the court system obtained a federal grant to develop a plan for a continuum of sanctions in domestic violence cases. Connecticut's law had provided for pretrial interventions, but had not created any specialized postconviction response. The planning grant included a set of in-depth interviews with battered women whose partners had been arrested. The interviews provided additional evidence that battered women, outside of a woman-defined safety planning advocacy model, often did not make a connection with advocates such that they felt their voices were heard in court. As plans were developed for sanctions, ways to enhance victims' safety and opportunities to be heard were incorporated.

These plans came to greater fruition with Connecticut's activities supported by Violence Against Women Act (VAWA) funding. In the first year of funding, a new advocate position was created that provided an opportunity to practice woman-defined safety planning and advocacy more fully. The new position was established in the context of a court where prosecutors identified "more serious" cases (those in which defendants had prior arrests for domestic violence or the instant offense involved weapons or substantial injury) for active prosecution.

These were cases in which there would be more extensive court contact with battered women, and safety issues would be paramount.

In less than a year, the woman-defined advocacy model had become the approach accepted and expected within that court. Advocates spent more time with women, and continued their involvement as the cases proceeded. Prosecutors requested advocates' participation in meetings with victims, and advocates met with women before and after meetings to help them understand their options and the legal process. Increasingly, battered women initiated contact with the advocates to ask questions, seek help, and provide updated information as their situations and preferences shifted. Advocates worked closely with court staff as well as community service providers, as they customized plans for services and interventions to suit the individual woman's hopes, needs, and concerns. As new protocols and approaches needed to be created along the way, advocates became active instigators of both individual and systemic change.

As this is being written, the woman-defined advocacy model has spread across the state in response to training and the expanded resources available with VAWA funding. Women's risk analysis has become a standard part of the training provided to all new advocates. Each court brings different challenges and opportunities, due to local histories and unique constellations of staff and perspectives. Wherever the model is adopted, however, better connections are forged between battered women and advocates and between advocates and the rest of the court staff. New legal and community intervention strategies continue to raise new questions, and court and community teams are created to develop solutions. The model itself changes with new issues and circumstances, as battered women's plans and perspectives do. Change for both individuals and systems is often a lengthy process, but effective woman-defined advocacy can accelerate the pace.

Notes

1. Contact was made in less than three quarters of the cases, largely due to inaccurate contact information and lack of time.

2. See, for example, Peled and Edleson (1994), who have noted a shift in attention by advocates toward a focus on individual causes of women's responses to their abuse.

3. Again, it must be stressed that these represent cumulative responses to limited resources. With expanded, coordinated service available, both women and support staff can and do take more action. See Hart (1992).

References

Abbott, J., Johnson, R., Koziol-McLain, J., & Lowenstein, S. (1995). Domestic violence against women: Incidence and prevalence in an emergency room population. *Journal of the American Medical Association, 273,* 1763-1767.

Adhikari, R., Reinhard, D., & Johnson, J. (1993). The myth of protective orders. *Studies in Symbolic Interaction, 15,* 259-270.

American Psychiatric Association. (1994). *Diagnostic and statistical manual of mental disorders* (4th ed.). Washington, DC: Author.

Arendell, T. (1995). *Fathers and divorce: At the intersection of family and gender.* Thousand Oaks, CA: Sage.

Astin, M., Lawrence, K., & Foy, D. (1993). Post-traumatic stress disorder among battered women: Risk and resiliency factors. *Violence and Victims, 8,* 17-28.

Bachman, R., & Coker, A. (1995). Police involvement in domestic violence: The interactive effects of victim injury, offender's history of violence, and race. *Violence and Victims, 10,* 91-106.

Barnett, O., & LaViolette, A. (1993). *It could happen to anyone.* Newbury Park, CA: Sage.

Bassuk, E. (1991). Homeless families. *Scientific American, 265,* 66-74.

Bassuk, E., & Rosenberg, L. (1988). Why does family homelessness occur? A case-control study. *American Journal of Public Health, 78,* 783-788.

Bassuk, E., Weinreb, L., Buckner, J., Browne, A., Salomon, A., & Bassuk, S. (1996). The characteristics and needs of sheltered homeless and low-income housed mothers. *Journal of the American Medical Association, 276,* 640-646.

Belknap, J., & McCall, K. (1994). Woman battering and police referrals. *Journal of Criminal Justice, 22,* 223-236.

Berk, S., & Loseke, D. (1980-1981). Handling family violence: Situational determinants of police arrest in domestic disturbances. *Law and Society Review, 50,* 317-346.

Better Homes Fund. (1994). *The Connecticut initiative on homelessness and family violence.* Hartford, CT: Connecticut Department of Public Health.

Blount, W., Silverman, I., Sellers, C., & Seese, R. (1994). Alcohol and drug use among abused women who kill, abused women who don't, and their abusers. *Journal of Drug Issues, 24,* 165-177.

Bograd, M. (1984). Family systems approaches to wife battering: A feminist critique. *American Journal of Orthopsychiatry, 54,* 558-568.

185

Bograd, M. (1988). How battered women and abusive men account for domestic violence: Excuses, justifications or explanations? In G. Hotaling, D. Finkelhor, & J. Kirkpatrick (Eds.), *Coping with family violence* (pp. 60-77). Newbury Park, CA: Sage.

Bowker, L. (1983). *Beating wife-beating.* Lexington, MA: Lexington Books.

Bowker, L., Arbitell, M., & McFarron, J. R. (1988). On the relationship between wife beating and wife abuse. In K. Yllo & M. Bograd (Eds.), *Feminist perspectives on wife abuse* (pp. 158-174). Newbury Park, CA: Sage.

Brown, J. (1997). Working toward freedom from violence: The process of change in battered women. *Violence Against Women, 3,* 5-26.

Browne, A. (1987). *When battered women kill.* New York: Free Press.

Bureau of Justice Statistics. (1994). *Selected findings: Violence between intimates* (NCJ-149259). Washington, DC: U.S. Department of Justice.

Buzawa, E., & Buzawa, C. (1990). *Domestic violence: The criminal justice response* (Studies in Crime, Law, and Justice, Vol. 6). Newbury Park, CA: Sage.

Buzawa, E., & Buzawa, C. (Eds.). (1993). The impact of arrest on domestic assault [Special issue]. *American Behavioral Scientist, 36.*

Buzawa, E., & Buzawa, C. (Eds.). (1996). *Do arrests and restraining orders work?* Thousand Oaks, CA: Sage.

Cahn, N., & Meier, J. (1995). Domestic violence and feminist jurisprudence: Towards a new agenda. *Public Interest Law Journal, 4,* 339-361.

Campbell, J. (1991). Public health conceptions of family abuse. In D. Knudsen & J. Miller (Eds.), *Abused and battered* (pp. 35-48). New York: Aldine de Gruyter.

Campbell, J. (1992). "If I can't have you, no one can": Power and control in homicide of female partners. In J. Radford & D. Russell (Eds.), *Femicide: The politics of woman killing* (pp. 99-113). New York: Twayne.

Campbell, J. (Ed.). (1995a). *Assessing dangerousness: Violence by sexual offenders, batterers, and child abusers.* Thousand Oaks, CA: Sage.

Campbell, J. (1995b). Prediction of homicide of and by battered women. In J. Campbell (Ed.), *Assessing dangerousness: Violence by sexual offenders, batterers, and child abusers* (pp. 96-113). Thousand Oaks, CA: Sage.

Campbell, J., Miller, P., Cardwell, M., & Belknap, R. (1994). Relationship status of battered women over time. *Journal of Family Violence, 9,* 99-111.

Campbell, R., Sullivan, C., & Davidson, W., II. (1995). Women who use domestic violence shelters: Changes in depression over time. *Psychology of Women Quarterly, 19,* 237-255.

Canadian Panel on Violence Against Women. (1993). *Changing the landscape: Ending violence—Achieving equality: Final report of the Canadian Panel on Violence Against Women.* Ottawa: Minister of Supply and Service.

Carlisle-Frank, P. (1991). Do battered women's beliefs about control affect their decisions to remain in abusive relationships? [Special issue]. *Violence Update, 1.*

Cazenave, N., & Straus, M. (1990). Race, class, network embeddedness, and family violence: A search for potent support systems. In M. Straus & R. Gelles (Eds.), *Physical violence in American families: Risk factors and adaptations to violence in 8,145 families* (pp. 321-329). New Brunswick, NJ: Transaction.

Chenoweth, L. (1996). Violence and women with disabilities: Silence and paradox. *Violence Against Women, 2,* 391-411.

Choice, P., Lamke, L., & Pittman, J. (1995). Conflict resolution strategies and marital distress as mediating factors in the link between witnessing interparental violence and wife battering. *Violence and Victims, 10,* 107-119.

Cook, D., & Frantz-Cook, A. (1984). A systemic treatment approach to wife-battering. *Journal of Marital and Family Therapy, 10,* 83-93.

Copelon, R. (1994). Intimate terror: Understanding domestic violence as torture. In R. Cook (Ed.), *Women's international human rights.* Philadelphia: University of Pennsylvania Press.

Crenshaw, K. (1994). Mapping the margins: Intersectionality, identity politics, and violence against women of color. In M. Fineman & B. Mykitiuk (Eds.), *The public nature of private violence* (pp. 93-118). New York: Routledge.

Crowell, N., & Burgess, A. (Eds.). (1996). *Understanding violence against women.* Washington, DC: National Academy Press.

Dasgupta, S. D., & Warrier, S. (1996). In the footsteps of "Arundhati": Asian Indian women's experience of domestic violence in the United States. *Violence Against Women, 2,* 238-259.

Davies, J. (1997). *The new welfare law: State implementation and use of the family violence option* (Welfare Issues and Domestic Violence Series, No. 2). Harrisburg, PA: National Resource Center on Domestic Violence.

Davis, L. (1987). Battered women: The transformation of a social problem. *Social Work, 32*(4), 306-311.

Davis, L., Hagen, J., & Early, T. (1994). Social services for battered women: Are they adequate, accessible, and appropriate? *Social Work, 39,* 695-704.

D'Ercole, A., & Struening, E. (1990). Victimization among homeless women: Implications for service delivery. *Journal of Community Psychology, 18,* 141-152.

Dobash, R. E., & Dobash, R. (1979). *Violence against wives: A case against the patriarchy.* New York: Free Press.

Dobash, R. E., & Dobash, R. P. (1992). *Women, violence and social change.* London and New York: Routledge.

Douglas, M. A. (1987). The battered woman syndrome. In D. Sonkin (Ed.), *Domestic violence on trial: Psychological and legal dimensions of family violence* (pp. 39-54). New York: Springer.

Dutton, D. (1988). *The domestic assault of women: Psychological and criminal justice perspectives.* Boston: Allyn & Bacon.

Dutton, D., & Painter, S. (1993). The battered woman syndrome: Effects of severity and intermittency of abuse. *American Journal of Orthopsychiatry, 63,* 614-622.

Dutton, M. A. (1992). *Empowering and healing the battered woman.* New York: Springer.

Dutton, M. A. (1996a). Battered women's strategic response to violence: The role of context. In J. Edleson & Z. Eisikovitz (Eds.), *Future interventions with battered women and their families* (pp. 105-124). Thousand Oaks, CA: Sage.

Dutton, M. A. (1996b). *The validity and use of evidence concerning battering and its effects in criminal trials.* Washington, DC: National Institute of Justice.

Eisikovits, Z., & Buchbinder, E. (1996). Pathways to disenchantment: Battered women's views of their social workers. *Journal of Interpersonal Violence, 11,* 425-440.

Ellis, D., & DeKeseredy, W. (1989). Marital status and woman abuse: The DAD model. *International Journal of Sociology of the Family, 19,* 67-87.

Ellis, D., & Stuckless, N. (1992). Preseparation, marital conflict mediation, and post-separation abuse. *Mediation Quarterly, 9,* 205-225.

Emerson, R. (1994). Constructing serious violence and its victims: Processing a domestic violence restraining order. In G. Miller & J. Holstein (Eds.), *Perspectives on social problems: A research manual* (Vol. 6). Greenwich, CT: JAI.

Employment and earnings. (1997, January). Washington, DC: U.S. Department of Labor, Bureau of Labor Statistics.

Federal Bureau of Investigation. (1993). *Uniform crime reports.* Washington, DC: U.S. Department of Justice.

Federal Bureau of Investigation. (1995). *Crime in the United States 1994.* Washington, DC: U.S. Department of Justice.

Ferraro, K. (1989). The legal response to woman battering in the United States. In J. Hanmer, J. Radford, & E. Stanko (Eds.), *Women, policing, and male violence* (pp. 155-184). London: Routledge.

Ferraro, K. (1993). Cops, courts, and woman battering. In P. Bart & E. Moran (Eds.), *Violence against women: The bloody footprints* (pp. 165-176). Newbury Park, CA: Sage.

Ferraro, K., & Johnson, J. (1983). How women experience battering: The process of victimization. *Social Problems, 30,* 325-339.

Finn, P., & Colson, S. (1990). *Civil protection orders: Legislation, current court practice, and enforcement.* Washington, DC: National Institute of Justice.

Finn, M., & Stalans, L. (1995). Police referrals to shelters and mental health treatment: Examining their decisions in domestic assault cases. *Crime & Delinquency, 41,* 467-480.

Fischer, K., & Rose, M. (1995). When "enough is enough": Battered women's decision making around court orders of protection. *Crime & Delinquency, 41,* 414-429.

Fleming, J. B. (1979). *Stopping wife abuse.* Garden City, NY: Anchor.

Follingstad, D., Hause, E., Rutledge, L., & Polek, D. (1992). Effects of battered women's early responses on later abuse patterns. *Violence and Victims, 7,* 109-128.

Follingstad, D., Rutledge, L., Berg, B., Hause, E., & Polek, D. (1990). The role of emotional abuse in physically abusive relationships. *Journal of Family Violence, 5,* 107-120.

Freeman, J. (1975). *The politics of women's liberation.* New York: David McKay.

Friedman, L., & Couper, S. (1987). *The cost of domestic violence: A preliminary investigation of the financial cost of domestic violence.* New York: Victim Services.

Frieze, I. (1979). Perceptions of battered wives. In I. Frieze, D. Bar-Tal, & J. Carroll (Eds.), *New approaches to social problems.* San Francisco: Jossey-Bass.

Fullerton, H. (1995). The 2005 labor force: Growing, but slowly. *Monthly Labor Review, 118,* 29-44.

Gelles, R. (1988). Violence and pregnancy: Are pregnant women at greater risk of abuse? *Journal of Marriage and the Family, 50,* 841-847.

Gelles, R., & Harrop, J. (1989). Violence, battering, and psychological distress among women. *Journal of Interpersonal Violence, 4,* 400-420.

Gelles, R., & Straus, M. (1988). *Intimate violence: The causes and consequences of abuse in the American family.* New York: Touchstone.

Giles-Sims, J. (1983). *Wife battering, a systems theory approach.* New York: Guilford.

Gleason, W. (1995). Children of battered women: Developmental delays and behavioral dysfunction. *Violence and Victims, 10,* 153-160.

Gondolf, E., & Fisher, E. (1988). *Battered women as survivors: An alternative to treating learned helplessness.* Lexington, MA: Lexington Books.

Goodman, L. (1991). The prevalence of abuse among homeless and housed poor mothers: A comparison study. *American Journal of Orthopsychiatry, 61,* 489-500.

Gordon, J. (1996). Community services for abused women: A review of perceived usefulness and efficacy. *Journal of Family Violence, 11,* 315-329.

Graham, D., Rawlings, E., & Rimini, N. (1988). Survivors of terror: Battered women, hostages and the Stockholm syndrome. In K. Yllo & M. Bograd (Eds.), *Feminist perspectives on wife abuse* (pp. 217-233). Newbury Park, CA: Sage.

Hagen, J. (1987). Gender and homelessness. *Social Work, 32,* 312-316.

Hampton, R., & Gelles, R. (1994). Violence toward black women in a nationally representative sample of black families. *Journal of Comparative Family Studies, 25,* 105-119.

Hansen, M., Harway, M., & Cervantes, N. (1991). Therapists' perceptions of severity in cases of family violence. *Violence and Victims, 6,* 225-235.

Hart, B. (1988). Beyond the "duty to warn": A therapist's "duty to protect" battered women and children. In K. Yllo & M. Bograd (Eds.), *Feminist perspectives on wife abuse* (pp. 234-248). Newbury Park, CA: Sage.

Hart, B. (1992). State codes on domestic violence [Special issue]. *Juvenile and Family Court Journal, 43.*

Helton, A., McFarlane, J., & Anderson, E. (1987). Battered and pregnant: A prevalence study. *American Journal of Public Health, 77,* 1337-1339.

Henderson, A. (1990). Children of abused wives: Their influence on their mothers' decisions. *Canada's Mental Health, 38,* 10-13.

Henning, K., Leitenberg, H., Coffey, P., Turner, T., & Bennett, R. (1996). Long-term psychological and social impact of witnessing physical conflict between parents. *Journal of Interpersonal Violence, 11,* 35-51.

Herbert, T., Silver, R., & Ellard, J. (1991). Coping with an abusive relationship: How and why do women stay? *Journal of Marriage and the Family, 53,* 311-325.

Hilton, N. Z. (1993). *Legal responses to wife assault.* Newbury Park, CA: Sage.

Hoff, L. (1990). *Battered women as survivors.* New York: Routledge.

Horton, A., & Johnson, B. (1993). Profile and strategies of women who have ended abuse. *Families in Society: The Journal of Contemporary Human Services, 74*(8), 481-492.

Horton, A., Simonidis, K., & Simonidis, L. (1987). Legal remedies for spousal abuse: Victim characteristics, expectations, and satisfaction. *Journal of Family Violence, 2,* 265-279.

Hotaling, G., & Sugarman, D. (1986). An analysis of risk markers in husband to wife violence: The current state of knowledge. *Violence and Victims, 1,* 101-124.

Houskamp, B., & Foy, D. (1991). The assessment of posttraumatic stress disorder in battered women. *Journal of Interpersonal Violence, 6,* 367-375.

Huisman, K. (1996). Wife battering in Asian American communities. *Violence Against Women, 2,* 260-283.

Jaffe, P., Wolfe, D., & Wilson, S. (1990). *Children of battered women.* Newbury Park, CA: Sage.

Jang, D. (1994). Caught in a web: Immigrant women and domestic violence. *Clearinghouse Review, 28,* 397-405.

Johnson, I. (1992). Economic, situational, and psychological correlates of the decision-making process of battered women. *Families in Society, 73,* 168-176.

Johnson, J. (1981). Program enterprise and official cooptation in the battered women's shelter movement. *American Behavioral Scientist, 24,* 827-842.

Johnson, J. (1992). Church responses to domestic violence. *Studies in Symbolic Interaction, 13,* 277-286.

Johnson, J., & Bondurant, D. (1992). Revisiting the 1982 church response survey. *Studies in Symbolic Interaction, 13,* 287-293.

Jones, A. (1994). *Next time she'll be dead.* Boston, MA: Beacon.

Kanuha, V. (1996). Domestic violence, racism, and the battered women's movement in the United States. In J. Edleson & Z. Eisikovits (Eds.), *Future interventions with battered women and their families* (pp. 34-50). Thousand Oaks, CA: Sage.

Kellermann, A., et al. (1993). Gun ownership as a risk factor for homicide in the home. *New England Journal of Medicine, 329,* 1084-1091.

Kelly, L. (1988). How women define their experiences of violence. In K. Yllo & M. Bograd (Eds.), *Feminist perspectives on wife abuse* (pp. 114-132). Newbury Park, CA: Sage.

Kelly, L. (1996). Tensions and possibilities: Enhancing informal responses to domestic violence. In J. Edleson & Z. Eisikovits (Eds.), *Future interventions with battered women and their families* (pp. 67-86). Thousand Oaks, CA: Sage.

Kemp, A., Green, B., Hovanitz, C., & Rawlings, E. (1995). Incidence and correlates of posttraumatic stress disorder in battered women. *Journal of Interpersonal Violence, 10,* 43-55.

Kirkwood, C. (1993). *Leaving abusive partners.* London: Sage.

Kleckner, J. (1978). Wife beaters and beaten wives: Co-conspirators in crimes and violence. *Psychology, 15,* 54-56.

Kolbo, J. (1996). Risk and resilience among children exposed to family violence. *Violence and Victims, 11,* 113-128.

Kolbo, J., Blakely, E., & Engleman, D. (1996). Children who witness domestic violence: A review of empirical literature. *Journal of Interpersonal Violence, 11,* 281-293.

Koss, M., Goodman, L., Browne, A., Fitzgerald, L., Keita, G., & Russo, N. (1994). *No safe haven: Male violence against women at home, at work, and in the community.* Washington, DC : American Psychological Association.

Kurz, D. (1987). Emergency department response to battered women: A case of resistance. *Social Problems, 34,* 501-513.

Kurz, D. (1995). *For richer, for poorer: Mothers confront divorce.* New York: Routledge.

Kurz, D. (1996). Separation, divorce, and woman abuse. *Violence Against Women, 2,* 63-81.

Layzer, J., Goodson, B., & deLange, C. (1986). Children in shelters. *Response to Victimization of Women and Children, 9,* 2-5.

Lempert, L. B. (1995). The line in the sand: Definitional dialogues in abusive relationships. *Studies in Symbolic Interaction, 18,* 171-195.

Lempert, L. B. (1996). Women's strategies for survival: Developing agency in abusive relationships. *Journal of Family Violence, 11,* 269-289.

Lerman, L. (1986). Prosecution of wife beaters: Institutional obstacles and innovations. In M. Lystad (Ed.), *Violence in the home: Interdisciplinary perspectives* (pp. 250-295). New York: Brunner/Mazel.

Limandri, B., & Sheridan, D. (1995). Prediction of intentional interpersonal violence: An introduction. In J. Campbell (Ed.), *Assessing dangerousness: Violence by sexual offenders, batterers, and child abusers* (pp. 1-19). Thousand Oaks, CA: Sage.

Liss, M., & Stahly, G. (1993). Domestic violence and child custody. In M. Hansen & M. Harway (Eds.), *Battering and family therapy: A feminist perspective* (pp. 175-187). Newbury Park, CA: Sage.

Loseke, D. (1992). *The battered woman and shelters: The social construction of wife abuse.* Albany: State University of New York Press.

Loving, N. (1980). *Responding to spouse abuse and wife beating: A guide for police.* Washington, DC: Police Executive Research Forum.

Lyon, E. (1993, August). *Deserving victims: The moral assessment of victims of crime.* Paper presented at the annual meeting of the Society for the Study of Social Problems, Miami.

Lyon, E., & Mace, P. (1989). *The Family Violence Prevention and Response Act: Services provided by the family violence victim advocates.* Report submitted to the State of Connecticut: Commission on Victim Services.

Lyon, E., & Mace, P. (1991). Family violence and the courts: Implementing a comprehensive new law. In D. Knudsen & J. Miller (Eds.), *Abused and battered* (pp. 167-179). New York: Aldine de Gruyter.

Mahoney, M. (1991). Legal images of battered women: Redefining the issue of separation. *Michigan Law Review, 90,* 1-94.

Mahoney, M. (1994). Victimization or oppression? Women's lives, violence, and agency. In M. Fineman & B. Mykitiuk (Eds.), *The public nature of private violence* (pp. 59-92). New York: Routledge.

Marden, M., & Rice, M. (1995). The use of hope as a coping mechanism in abused women. *Journal of Holistic Nursing, 13,* 70-82.

McFarlane, J., Parker, K., Soeken, K., & Bullock, L. (1992). Assessing abuse during pregnancy: Severity and frequency of injuries and associated entry into prenatal care. *Journal of the American Medical Association, 267,* 3176-3178.

McKeel, A. J., & Sporakowski, M. J. (1993). How shelter counselors' views about responsibility for wife abuse relate to services they provide to battered women. *Journal of Family Violence, 8,* 101-112.

McKibben, L., DeVos, E., & Newberger, E. (1989). Victimization of mothers of abused children: A controlled study. *Pediatrics, 84,* 531-535.

McLeer, S., & Anwar, R. (1989). A study of battered women presenting in an emergency department. *American Journal of Public Health, 79,* 65-66.

Miller, B., Downs, W., & Gondoli, D. (1989). Spousal violence among alcoholic women as compared to a random household sample of women. *Journal of Studies on Alcohol, 50,* 533-540.

Mills, T. (1985). The assault on the self: Stages in coping with battering husbands. *Qualitative Sociology, 8,* 103-123.

NiCarthy, G. (1987). *The ones who got away: Women who left abusive partners.* Seattle, WA: Seal.

O'Brien, K., & Murdock, N. (1993). Shelter workers' perceptions of battered women. *Sex Roles, 29,* 183-194.

O'Keefe, M. (1994). Adjustment of children from maritally violent homes. *Families in Society, 75*(7), 403-415.

O'Keefe, M. (1995). Predictors of child abuse in maritally violent families. *Journal of Interpersonal Violence, 10,* 3-25.

O'Keefe, M. (1997). Incarcerated battered women: A comparison of battered women who killed their abusers and those incarcerated for other offenses. *Journal of Family Violence, 12,* 1-19.

Okun, L. (1986). *Woman abuse: Facts replacing myths.* Albany: State University of New York Press.

Orloff, L., Jang, D., & Klein, C. (1995). With no place to turn: Improving legal advocacy for battered immigrant women. *Family Law Quarterly, 29,* 313-329.

Osofsky, J. (1995). Children who witness domestic violence: The invisible victims. *Social Policy Report, 9*(3), 1-16.

Pagelow, M. (1981). *Woman battering: Victims and their experiences.* Beverly Hills, CA: Sage.

Peled, E. (1996). "Secondary" victims no more: Refocusing intervention with children. In J. Edleson & Z. Eisikovits (Eds.), *Future interventions with battered women and their families* (pp. 125-153). Thousand Oaks, CA: Sage.

Peled, E., & Edleson, J. (1994). Advocacy for battered women: A national survey. *Journal of Family Violence, 9,* 285-296.

Peled, E., Jaffe, P., & Edleson, J. (Eds.). (1995). *Ending the cycle of violence: Community responses to children of battered women.* Thousand Oaks, CA: Sage.

Perilla, J., Bakeman, R., & Norris, F. (1994). Culture and domestic violence: The ecology of abused Latinas. *Violence and Victims, 9,* 325-339.

Rauma, D. (1984). Going for the gold: Prosecutorial decision making in cases of wife assault. *Social Science Research, 13,* 32-51.

Renzetti, C. (1992). *Violent betrayal: Partner abuse in lesbian relationships.* Newbury Park, CA: Sage.

Richie, B. (1996). *Compelled to crime: The gender entrapment of battered black women.* New York: Routledge.

Rigakos, G. (1995). Constructing the symbolic complainant: Police subculture and the nonenforcement of protection orders for battered women. *Violence and Victims, 10,* 227-247.

Salts, C. (1979). Divorce process: Integration of theory. *Journal of Divorce, 2,* 233-240.

Saunders, D. (1995). The tendency to arrest victims of domestic violence: A preliminary analysis of officer characteristics. *Journal of Interpersonal Violence, 10,* 147-158.

Schechter, S. (1982). *Women and male violence.* Boston, MA: South End.

Seavey, D. (1996). *Back to basics: Women's poverty and welfare reform.* Wellesley, MA: Wellesley College, Center for Research on Women.

Seligman, M. E. P. (1975). *Helplessness: On depression, development and death.* San Francisco: Freeman.

Shainess, N. (1977). Psychological aspects of wife-battering. In M. Roy (Ed.), *Battered women* (pp. 111-119). New York: Van Nostrand Reinhold.

Sherman, L., & Berk, R. (1984). The specific deterrent effects of arrests for domestic assault. *American Sociological Review, 49,* 261-272.

Shields, N., & Hanneke, C. (1983). Battered wives' reactions to marital rape. In D. Finkelhor, R. Gelles, G. Hotaling, & M. Straus (Eds.), *The dark side of families: Current family violence research* (pp. 131-148). Beverly Hills, CA: Sage.

Sorenson, S., Upchurch, D., & Shen, H. (1996). Violence and injury in marital arguments. *American Journal of Public Health, 86,* 35-40.

Stalans, L., & Finn, M. (1995). How novice and experienced officers interpret wife assaults: Normative and efficiency frames. *Law and Society Review, 29,* 287-321.

Stark, E., & Flitcraft, A. (1995). Killing the beast within: Woman battering and female suicidality. *International Journal of Health Sciences, 25,* 43-64.

Stark, E., Flitcraft, A., & Frazier, W. (1979). Medicine and patriarchal violence: The social construction of a private event. *International Journal of Health Services, 9,* 461-492.

Stark, E., & Flitcraft, A. (1988). Women and children at risk: A feminist perspective on child abuse. *International Journal of Health Services, 18,* 97-118.

Straus, M. (1983). Ordinary violence, child abuse, and wife-beating: What do they have in common? In D. Finkelhor, R. Gelles, G. Hotaling, & M. Straus (Eds.), *The dark side of families: Current family violence research* (pp. 213-234). Beverly Hills, CA: Sage.

Straus, M., & Gelles, R. (1986). Societal change and change in family violence from 1975 to 1985 as revealed by two national surveys. *Journal of Marriage and the Family, 48,* 465-479.

Strube, M. (1988). The decision to leave an abusive relationship: Empirical evidence and theoretical issues. *Psychological Bulletin, 104,* 236-250.

Strube, M., & Barbour, L. (1983). The decision to leave an abusive relationship: Economic dependence and psychological commitment. *Journal of Marriage and the Family, 45,* 785-793.

Suh, E., & Abel, E. (1990). The impact of spousal violence on the children of the abused. *Journal of Independent Social Work, 4,* 27-34.

Sullivan, C. (1991). The provision of advocacy services to women leaving abusive partners. *Journal of Interpersonal Violence, 6,* 41-54.

Tierney, K. (1982). The battered women movement and the creation of the wife beating problem. *Social Problems, 29,* 207-220.

Walker, L. (1979). *The battered woman.* New York: Harper & Row.

Walker, L. (1984). *The battered woman syndrome.* New York: Springer.

Walker, L. (1991). Post-traumatic stress disorder in women: Diagnosis and treatment of battered woman syndrome. *Psychotherapy, 28,* 21-29.

Walker, L., & Edwall, G. (1987). Domestic violence and determination of visitation and custody in divorce. In D. Sonkin (Ed.), *Domestic violence on trial: Psychological and legal dimensions of family violence* (pp. 127-154). New York: Springer.

Warshaw, C. (1993). Limitations of the medical model in the care of battered women. In P. Bart & E. Moran (Eds.), *Violence against women: The bloody footprints* (pp. 134-146). Newbury Park, CA: Sage.

Warshaw, C., & Ganley, A. (1995). *Improving the health care response to domestic violence: A resource manual for health care providers.* San Francisco: Family Violence Prevention Fund.

Websdale, N. (1995). Rural woman abuse. *Violence Against Women, 1,* 309-338.

Whalen, M. (1996). *Counseling to end violence against women: A subversive model.* Thousand Oaks, CA: Sage.

White, J., & Koss, M. (1991). Courtship violence: Incidence in a national sample of higher education students. *Violence and Victims, 6,* 247-256.

Wiseman, R. (1975). Crisis theory—The process of divorce. *Social Casework, 56,* 205-212.

Wood, D., Valdez, R., Hayashi, T., & Shin, A. (1990). Homeless and housed families in Los Angeles: A study comparing demographic, economic, and family function characteristics. *American Journal of Public Health, 80,* 1049-1052.

Index

About the Authors

Jill Davies is an attorney who works on a local, state, and national level to improve the legal response to family violence and to enhance advocacy for battered women. She has trained extensively on family violence and legal issues, with a focus on effective advocacy in the legal sysgtem and the effects of the legal system's response on battered women's safety planning. Attorney Davies serves on several state and national advisory boards regarding family violence and is a consultant to the National Resource Center on Domestic Violence. Attorney Davies is currently the deputy director of Greater Hartford Legal Assistance, Inc. Attorney Davies has written numerous pieces about family violence. Recent work includes: A series of papers about the new federal welfare law and domestic violence, developed for the National Resource Center on Domestic Violence, *Violence Against Women Act State Implementation Plan Development; An Approach to Legtal Advocacy for Individual Battered Women,* and the *Connecticut Family Violence Victim Advocate Resource Manual,* second edition.

Eleanor Lyon, Ph.D., has directed research, planning, and evaluation efforts related to battered women and family violence at the national, state, and local level since 1981. Prior to that, she served as director of a local battered women's shelter in Connecticut. She has worked collaboratively with policymakers and service providers on several projects to improve the legal system's response to domestic violence; she has also conducted multiple studies of alternatives to incarceration. She is a research consultant to the National Resource Center on Domestic Violence, and has provided technical assistance to the National Institute of Corrections. She is a deputy editor of the *Journal of Contemporary Ethnography,* for which she recently edited a special issue on applied ethnography. She has trained and presented extensively at national and international conferences, and written articles and reports on her research with battered women and the effect of mandatory arrest. She is currently a Research Associate at the Village for Families & Children in Hartford, where she specializes in qualitative research methods and violence against women. She is also an adjunct Professor of Sociology at the University of Connecticut's Hartford campus.

Diane Monti-Catania is a nationally recognized training specialist in the area of violence against women. She has been an advocate for battered women since 1982. Ms. Monti-Catania works with domestic violence and sexual assault coalitions throughout the country developing training programs for law enforcement on responding to violence against women. Her recent writing includes: "Violence Against Women and HIV/AIDS," in *The Gender Politics of HIV/AIDS: Police Response to Crimes of Domestic Violence in Connecticut; Police Response to Crimes of Sexual Violence in Pennsylvania;* and *Court Advocate Manual for Maryland Sexual Assault Advocates.* She is the founder of The Advocacy Institute, LLC, a consulting firm dedicated to social change through education and planning. The current focus of her work is improving institutional and community response to violence against women, poverty, and HIV/AIDS.